Making Stringed Instruments

A Workshop Guide

Making Stringed Instruments

A Workshop Guide

George Buchanan

Sterling Publishing Co., Inc.   New York

Library of Congress Cataloging-in-Publication Data

Buchanan, George.
   [Making of stringed instruments]
   Making stringed instruments: a workshop guide / George Buchanan.
     p. cm.
   Originally published: The making of stringed instruments.
   Includes bibliographical references and index.
    1. Stringed instruments. Bowed—Construction.   2. Mandolin—
Construction.   3. Mandola—Construction.   4. Guitar—Construction.
I. Title.
ML755.B78 1990
787′.1923—dc20   90–9952
                                        CIP
                                       MN

10 9 8 7 6 5 4 3 2

Published in 1990 by Sterling Publishing Company, Inc.
387 Park Avenue South, New York, N.Y. 10016
Originally published in Great Britain by B. T. Batsford, Ltd
as *The Making of Stringed Instruments* © 1989 by George Buchanan
Distributed in Canada by Sterling Publishing
c/o Canadian Manda Group, P.O. Box 920, Station U
Toronto, Ontario, Canada M8Z 5P9
Printed and Bound in Great Britain
All rights reserved

Sterling ISBN 0–8069–7464–8

To Uncle Bo

Acknowledgements

I wish to thank David Buchanan for the inspiration and guidance he has given me; Peter Harding for these magnificent photographs; and Elizabeth for her invaluable help and encouragement.

Contents

Introduction

This book provides a simple and concise account of the steps and processes necessary to make a violin, viola, cello, mandolin, mandola and guitar (jazz and classical), with some hints and ideas to encourage the faint-hearted and bolster the confidence of those who have had little experience in the use of hand tools.

To some this may seem an impossible objective. Musical instruments reflect the consummate art and skill of the master who fashioned them, an expertise that cannot be learnt quickly, and that requires many unusual skills. Yet whoever begins to make stringed instruments will find that the challenge is exciting. They will quickly become addicted to the craft's peculiar fascination, and they will find that they have discovered a hobby of a lifetime.

Part I:

The Workshop

The Workshop

The instrument maker's workshop does not need to be large; you just need room for a small bench or table and a pair of long trestles. Make sure you have good general lighting but, as diffused light does not show up surface irregularites, supplement it with a swing arm lamp, which can be directed at the workpiece while it is being carved.

The workshop should be warm and dry to avoid problems of shrinkage once the instrument is assembled. Hide glue is used hot for all the assembly work and must not chill before joints are assembled. In a small room a portable gas heater is satisfactory, but it is better to use a wood-burning stove which will dispose of the waste shavings and chippings.

Clean the workshop between operations and before tools or worksurfaces are covered in shavings. I enjoy the smell of freshly cut wood, particularly if pine or cedar are being worked, but you may lose things in the shavings and the dust from them makes cleaning up and varnishing very difficult.

Keep the workshop tidy. Fit shelves near the workbench and stack them with freezer boxes of components and tools. Mark the contents of each box. Hang screw top bottles beneath the shelves and store nails, pins, rubber bands and other small items in them. Hang violin clamps from the shelves. Some suggestions for hooking tools to the toolboard fixed to the wall over the workbench are pictured in the illustration.

Moulds and the carving box can be pinned to the wall. Cover partially completed instruments in plastic bags or store them in a cupboard to keep them clean. Ready-cut violin making woods should be stored in the workshop with matched boards bound together with masking tape. Techniques for storing larger pieces of wood outside the workshop are described later.

General tools

The following section describes the tools that you need. You may have to make some of these, and buy other specialist ones.

Ripsaw

This is a handsaw, used for cutting along the grain of a piece of wood. It is held as illustrated. The teeth, which are sharpened at right-angles to the blade, cut with a chiselling action on the push stroke.

Sharpening

A dull ripsaw bounces in the cut, and roars and grinds away without any satisfying sense of progress, whereas a sharp saw crackles as it bites through the wood. Inspect the blade by holding the teeth to the light. A dull blade will reflect light from the teeth points.

move freely through the wood and permits a little latitude in which to alter the direction of the cut. As you become more proficient in using the saw, less set is needed and sawing becomes an easier and quicker operation.

Once the teeth have been set, clamp the saw between a pair of substantial saw cheeks to hold the blade steady, and fix it in the vice. Take a new, small, saw sharpening file and file the teeth to shape. Three passes of the file are usually enough to remove the flats left by the tipping file and bring the teeth back into shape. When all the teeth have been sharpened, place the blade flat on the table and run a sharpening stone lightly down each side, working from the tip to the handle to remove any swarf left by the files and lower badly set teeth.

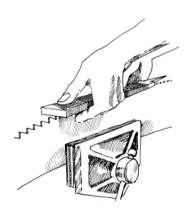

To set the teeth, hold a file perpendicular to the blade, and run it over the teeth, nipping off the top of the teeth, until they are all the same height. Set the teeth using a saw set adjusted to the number of teeth per inch of the saw. Bend the teeth off centre on alternate sides. This gives the saw clearance (kerf) and allows it to

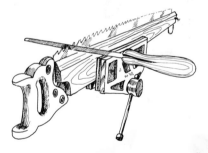

Crosscut saws

These saws have smaller teeth, sharpened like small knives, which sever the grain when cutting across a plank. Use a crosscut saw like a ripsaw, but follow a knife cut rather than a pencil line, as the grain tends to tear out as the blade passes through the wood, leaving a ragged edge. The knife cut weakens the surface fibres of the wood and prevents this.

Sharpening

Once the teeth have been tipped and set, hold the file at 60 degrees and sharpen alternate teeth. Each pass of the file sharpens the trailing edge on one tooth and the leading edge of the next. Work from the tip, and when one side is finished, rotate the saw in the vice and work up the other side, starting from the tip. Each side of the saw should be sharpened with previously unused file faces, held at a steady angle and with the same number of strokes per tooth. This prevents new irregularities being introduced into the teeth of the saw.

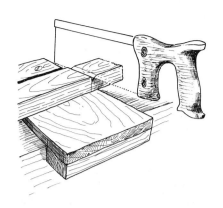

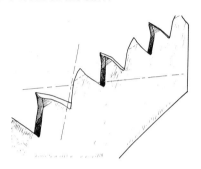

accuracy, start the horizontal cut, and then quickly bias the saw down the vertical side of the wood until the blade is cutting at 45 degrees to both surfaces. When the line is established, work the saw until the blade leads with its tip downwards.

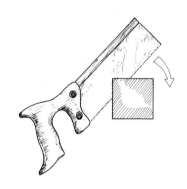

Backsaw

This is a small, fine-bladed rigid saw, with tiny teeth, used for short precise cuts. It is often used in conjuction with a bench hook (see page 26). To guarantee an accurate and clean cut when working across the grain, relieve the waste side of the scribe line with a knife and chisel before cutting. To achieve vertical

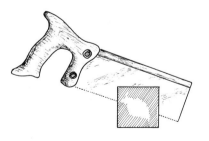

Sharpening
This is the same as the crosscut saw, except that it is unnecessary to set each tooth. Very little clearance is required on such narrow blades, especially where the teeth are small and the wood is hard and dry. Set every four or so teeth before sharpening, working from both sides with the saw file held at about 75 degrees.

Coping saw

If you don't have a bandsaw, you will need a coping saw to cut out the neck, scroll and around the outsides of the back and belly of the instrument. This saw is held as illustrated.

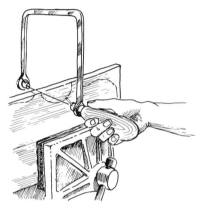

Blades are replaceable and are clipped into swivels at the ends of the sprung steel frame, which, when rotated, permit the blade to cut complex shapes without having to reposition the saw. Difficulties in using this saw occur if the swivels are incorrectly aligned, causing the blade to wander and twist, or the blade has become dull and needs replacing.

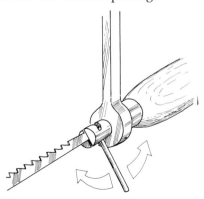

Scroll saw

This saw can be fitted with a variety of fine blades. The saw has a deep throat, which allows work to be rotated while the blade cuts in a constant direction. Hold the saw as illustrated, cutting on the downward stroke. Only the slightest vertical movement is necessary. Use a special sawing table to support flimsy work.

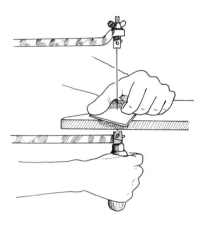

The lines scribed on the table indicate the position of the centre of the V and are a help when the workpiece is large and obscures parts of the table.

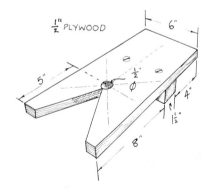

Chisels and gouges

Three bevel-edged chisels are needed: ¼ in, ⅜ in, and ⅝ in. You can make smaller chisels when required. Three gouges are also needed,

15

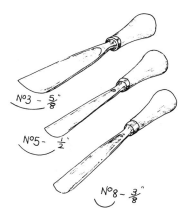

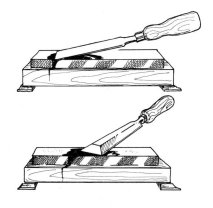

illustrated above. They should all have smooth and comfortable handles. File and sandpaper away any hard edges or roughness before using them. As gouges are the most important tools used in violin making, they must always be sharp – not to take bigger bites but for easier manipulation. Violin making is a delicate and skilful craft, and it is difficult to accomplish careful and clean work if the tools need massive force to drive them.

Use both hands to hold these tools. One hand grips the blade close to the cutting edge and guides and restrains the tool, while the other hand, often lodged against your chest as you lean into the work, applies forward thrust. Each cut should remove its own shaving. Never use these tools single-handed.

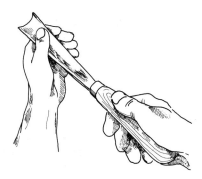

Sharpening chisels

Sharpen these to a 15-20 degree sharpening angle. Hold the tool rigidly at this angle and pass it back and forth over the rough face of an oilstone, until a burr is raised on the flat of the chisel. Lubricate the stone with oil when necessary. Once a burr has been raised, turn it over and clean it away, holding the chisel flat against the stone. Repeat, using less pressure, until a second burr is raised. Remove this and then move to a finer stone, and repeat two more times, reducing hand-pressure but maintaining the angle of the tool. Finish by removing the burr and then stropping the blade on a leather strop impregnated with stropping compound available from your barber – five times on the sharpening edge and once on the flat. If the strop is kept handy and used every few minutes, the chisel will remain keen for a long time.

Sharpening gouges

The process is similar to that described for chisels except that, since it is impossible to remove the inside burr on a flat oilstone, a slip stone is needed. Gouges can be ground on the same oilstone as the chisels and plane blades,

TWIST THE GOUGE AS IT MOVES ACROSS THE STONE.

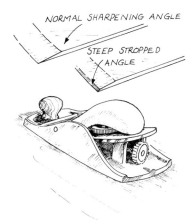

but because they gradually cut a depression in the surface of the stone, they spoil it for sharpening the flat-edged tools. Buy a slipstone which is big enough to sharpen the gouge on its side and let a groove develop there which, as it deepens, facilitates honing the outer bevel of the gouge. The illustrations show the procedure for sharpening the gouges. Make a stropping board from waste wood with grooves and profiles, smeared with compound, cut in its surface. Keep this beside the workpiece and use it every few minutes.

Planes

You will need some small violin maker's planes; these are described in detail with instructions for making later in this chapter. If the reader has a long plane, or can buy one cheaply secondhand, then it will save him some time. Otherwise, it is best to invest in one very good quality small block plane (as illustrated) and use that for all of the work.

If the plane is bought new, inspect it carefully and remove any sharp edges on the plane sole and hand holds with a file and abrasive paper. This will prevent the plane scoring the surface that has been carefully smoothed, and makes it more comfortable to hold. Sharpen the blade to the same low angle as the chisels and set the plane so that very little blade is showing.

The low angle block plane is probably the most versatile of the planes used in woodwork and, provided that the workpieces are resting on a firm, level surface, it should be easy to smooth and level with. However, when planing hardwoods, particularly those with complex grain patterns, the blade may tend to lever the grain up as it glides across the surface. To avoid this, lubricate the sole of the plane with candle wax; this enables you to adopt a lighter and more sensitive touch. In addition, remove the blade, and strop a different, steeper sharpening angle, which should reduce its tendency to tear the wood.

Adze

Curved sculptor's adzes are available from good tool shops and from the mail order companies listed in the back of the book. They are very useful for removing waste wood from inside the back and belly of the instrument. They are sharpened exactly like a gouge, and must be at least as sharp. For violin making, the trick is to cut across the grain and to allow the weight of the adzehead to carry the blade through its stroke. Practise on waste wood making fairly rapid cuts, each cut releasing its

17

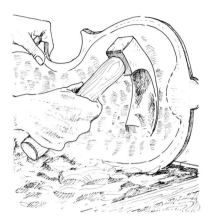

own shaving; try to keep all the shavings about the same size. This tool is particularly useful, not only because it is speedy, but because it allows you to adopt a relaxed posture once you are confident in your aim.

Reamer

One reamer is required for tapering the peg holes and the hole for the end pin in the base of the instrument. Reamers can become congested with wood dust, and will need to be withdrawn regularly and cleaned with a pointed stick run down each cutter. When they become dull, they can be honed with a small slipstone.

Clamps

A selection of clamps is always useful. Two bar clamps and four large C-clamps are really the minimum necessary. Use these with protective pads on their faces to prevent marking the work.

Homemade and specialist tools

All of the tools in the following section can be purchased, though perhaps in a slightly different form. However, for the sake of economy and experimentation, I have included instructions for making these simple tools at home.

Scrapers

A variety of shapes is required, some of which are illustrated. Scrapers are easy to make and to

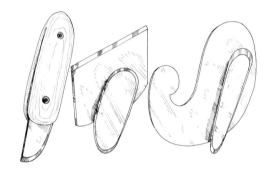

use, provided that they are sharp and conform roughly to the shape desired. Hold the scraper lightly and draw it over the surface of the timber. The fine cutting hook will remove the high spots and level the surface. Scrapers work best with the grain, but can, with care, be used in most situations.

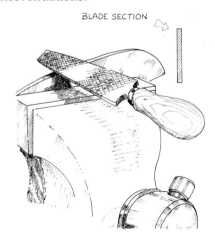

BLADE SECTION

Scrapers are made from thin sheets of tool steel, available in standard sizes from tool stores. They do not need to be more than $1/16$ in

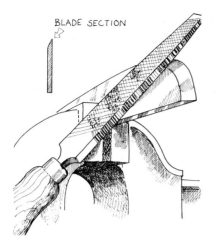

BLADE SECTION

thick, but it seems that the thicker scrapers, though less versatile, are nicer to handle and hold their edges longer. File the edge to the desired profile, then file a sharpening angle along its edge. Hone this in exactly the same way as a chisel or plane blade, flatting off the burr several times, and finish with a leather strop. Then take a hardened steel burnishing iron (the back of a gouge is satisfactory) and with a single pass, work a hook at the edge. The steel should not be tempered, so shapes can be changed whenever necessary. As the scraper begins to dull, the burnishing iron can be used to flatten back the hook, which is then reworked exactly as before. This can be done several times before the hook weakens and needs to be completely resharpened. Fit handles to the scrapers you find the most useful.

BLADE SECTION

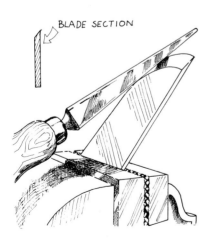

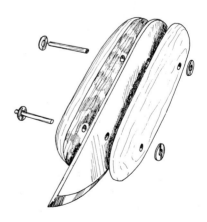

Screw gauge

The simple screw gauge illustrated is used to scribe a thickness line round the edge of the back and belly once the outlines of these parts have been cut out. Adjust the setting by turning the screw.

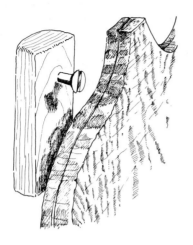

Safety razor blades

It is useful to have a supply of sharp safety razor blades handy when preparing the instrument for its final sanding. Sometimes it will be an advantage to work a hook at the edge of the blade. Its flexibility enables the blade to function in difficult corners around the neck, and over the purfling, where it can clean areas that are hard to reach with bigger, stiffer tools.

Flexible rasp

This is an unusual but very effective tool   is made from four to six good quality hacksaw blades, laid side by side with their teeth pointing in alternate directions. Bind their ends together with masking tape. It is used like a scraper and bent as it is pushed diagonally over the wood. This is an ideal tool for removing large irregularities in the surface of the back or belly, before finishing with a scraper.

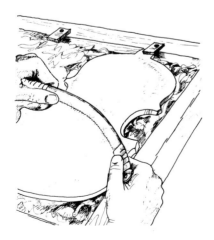

Large reamer

This will be needed only for fitting a spike in the end block of a cello. It is made from a tempered tool steel blade, set in a tapered length of hardwood. The hardwood barrel is turned or carved to conform to the taper of the insert that clamps the cello spike, and is then slotted to receive the blade, which is roughened before being glued

in place with hide glue. A hole is drilled through the head to take a tommy bar. This is used in exactly the same way as the peg reamer, but as this tool has only a single blade and a wooden shaft, it has to be handled gently.

Chisels

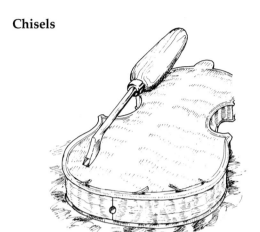

For most of the time, the three bevel-edged chisels and the gouges mentioned above will be quite sufficient. However, a very fine chisel is necessary to clear the groove which is cut to take the inlaid decoration around the edge of the instrument. This is an easy tool to make and, by doing so, you can change and adapt the tool when required. Use a 3/32 in rod of tool steel and cut it to length. File a tang at one end, and heat, bend and hammer the other end as

illustrated. Use small files to shape the cutting edge, until it is the same width as the purfling. Then file a sharpening angle on its upper edge. Temper this edge by heating it until it is cherry red; then dunk the blade immediately into cooking oil. Clean the cutting edge with steel wool and reheat it. When the metal at the tip begins to turn blue, stop heating, and allow the steel to cool. To fit the handle, place the shaft of the blade in the vice. Heat the tang with a blow-torch. When it is red hot, place the wooden handle over the tang and tap it down. Hone the chisel in the normal way.

Planes

Three small planes will be needed. Although expensive to buy, they are enjoyable and easy to make. The illustrations show the size of the three planes.

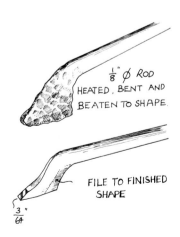

$\frac{1}{8}$" ø ROD HEATED, BENT AND BEATEN TO SHAPE.

FILE TO FINISHED SHAPE

$\frac{3}{64}$"

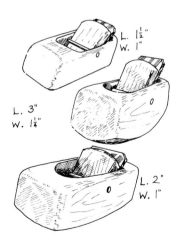

L. $1\frac{1}{2}$"
W. 1"

L. 3"
W. $1\frac{1}{4}$"

L. 2"
W. 1"

21

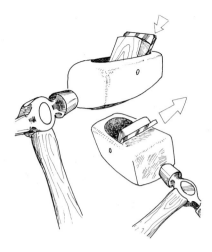

The plane iron is retained by the wedge which bears against the rod crossing the slot in the middle of the body. To lower the blade, tap the plane on its nose with a light hammer. A light knock on its back will raise the blade. These planes are used in the palm of the hand, so should be smooth and easy to hold.

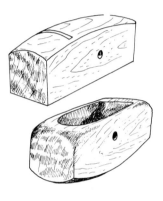

loose. Make a wedge from some suitable scrap of hardwood, then make the blade in exactly the same way that the scrapers are made, and harden it before honing.

Select a small block of boxwood, beech, sycamore or other hardwood; cut it to size and hollow the slot for the plane iron. Level this with a file and drill the hole for the blade-retaining rod, which can be made from the mild steel shaft of a 4 inch nail. Shape the sole and sides, and the top of the plane, and insert the rod, roughening its ends to stop it working

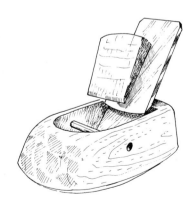

When designing your own planes, bear in mind that with only a wedge to hold the blade, and a fairly wide mouth to the slot, it is best to avoid experimenting with low angle cutting irons.

Purfling tool

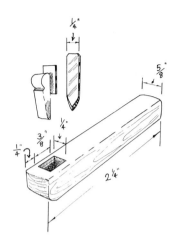

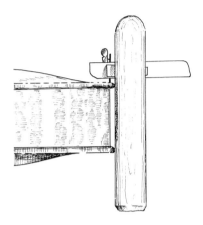

This is used to mark the line for the inlay fitted around the edges of the instrument. Purfling tools can be bought, but they are easy to make and just as satisfactory. The tool illustrated will be suitable for violin and viola making. With the fence reversed, it will bear against the back and belly of a cello and mark the purfling there too.

The tool is held lightly in the right hand, with the fence resting against the edges of the back and belly, and the point of the knife touching the surface of the instrument. By moving the tool, and sometimes the instrument, and with gentle pressure on the stock, the knife will follow the edge and cut a neat incised line. In the section on pages 89-95 more detail will be given of the process of inlaying the instrument. Remember, however, that this is a marker and not a router to excavate the groove for the purfling; at the corners and the button, for instance, it is useless, as the line of the inlay deviates from the outer edges of the instrument.

Use straight-grained hardwood for this tool and make it substantial so that it is easy and comfortable to hold. The stock is a short length

of rectangular hardwood of regular section, with a vertical slot for the blade and wedge. The fence, which is bigger, has a mortice which passes through it and two slots for holding the wedge. The face sides of the fence are hollowed slightly, to give it stability when working around curves. The fence, the stock and the wedges must all be tight fits, as changes to the adjustments are made only once for each instrument, and the adjustments must not slip accidentally. Make the blade from a small jigsaw blade, or from tool steel specially hardened. Hone it on one side only. Fit a neat hardwood wedge to hold the blade.

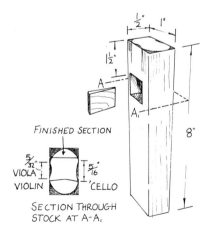

FINISHED SECTION

VIOLA
VIOLIN
'CELLO

SECTION THROUGH
STOCK AT A-A₁

Calipers

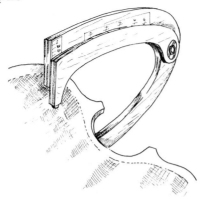

This is a homemade alternative to the more accurate, expensive dial gauge, and quite as suitable. It is made from two sheets of ⅜ in ply, and pivots on a large diameter bolt. Provided that its bearing faces do not wear, it is accurate enough. Calibrate the gauge once it is assembled. You can make a quick read-off scale, as well as a more accurate scale at its jaws.

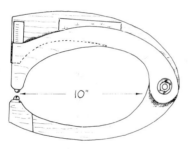

Clamp

The illustrations show a variety of useful clamps. Screw clamps are essential for assembling the body of the instrument. The

threaded rod (studding) is available from most hardware stores. A minimum of six will be required. Simple steel hand-grips are invaluable, particularly if you prefer to work alone. Lining clamps made from wooden clothes pegs are useful and cheap, which is good, as lots are needed.

BASS BAR CLAMP

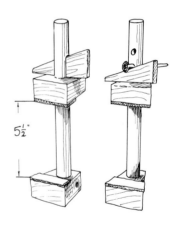

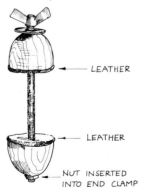

LEATHER

LEATHER

NUT INSERTED INTO END CLAMP

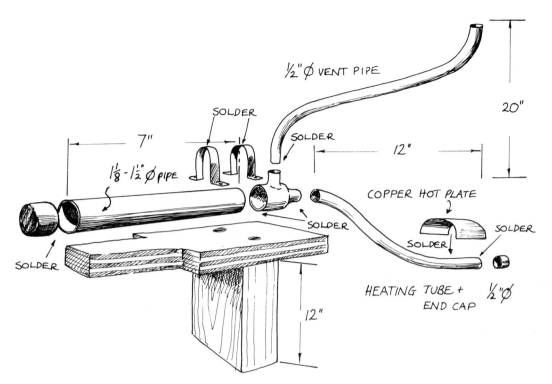

½" ⌀ VENT PIPE

20"

SOLDER

SOLDER

7"

12"

1⅛ - 1½ ⌀ PIPE

COPPER HOT PLATE

SOLDER

SOLDER

SOLDER

SOLDER

SOLDER

HEATING TUBE + END CAP

½" ⌀

12"

Bending iron

Electric and gas bending irons are available and are perfectly satisfactory, but they are costly. Anyone who posesses an electrician's soldering iron, of about 40 watts rating, can make a simple bending iron by carving two wooden blocks to grip the handle, and then slipping a small-diameter copper tube onto the barrel of the iron.

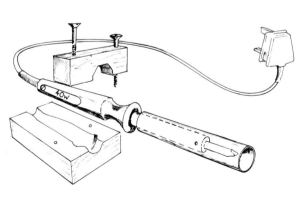

Clamp the iron to the side of the workbench. When it is switched on, the tube will become extremely hot, and is ideal for bending the thicker sides and linings used in guitar and mandolin construction.

The illustration shows how a few short lengths of plumbing tube, joints and two caps can be assembled to make a very effective and cheap alternative. Once assembled pour a small quantity of water into the vent pipe; this percolates to the end of the narrow tube. The narrow tube is heated, the water boils and steam travels into the larger tube, which heats up. The long vent tube condenses the steam. Occasionally, you have to replenish the water. For those who are not familiar with plumbing techniques, the key to successful jointing is to clean all jointing surfaces very carefully then to apply flux with a stick, and thereafter to refrain from handling the joints. Assemble the pieces and play a blow torch over each joint until the solder in the fittings melts and a line of solder appears at the joint. When using this bender, ensure that shavings and chippings are cleared away to avoid fire hazard.

Carving box

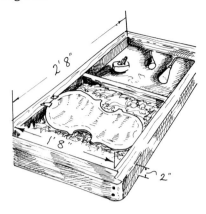

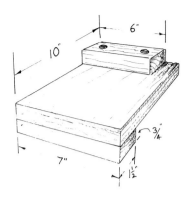

The carving box illustrated is long enough to hold the back of the cello and wide enough to hold a violin or a viola. Small leather or wooden buttons hold the edge of the workpiece, which rests in the box on a soft layer of shavings. The most arduous part of the process of making instruments is the hollowing out of the backs, and this is the best way that I have been able to devise for holding them, whilst I straddle the trestles and carve away in relative discomfort.

Bench hook

This simple jig is useful for holding a workpiece when sawing or chiselling on the bench. If, on one side, the hook is planed accurately and fitted at right angles to the main cutting board, its second side can double as a small shooting board.

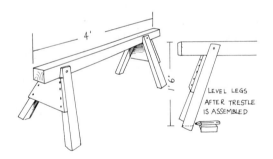

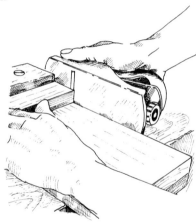

Trestles

The drawings show the dimensions and construction details of a simple trestle. Trim the tops and bottoms of the legs once the trestle is assembled.

Shooting board

This is a simple jig which provides a true edge, and a square support which is useful when planing a straight and square side to a board that is to be joined. A shooting board is particularly useful when shooting the joints to the back of a mandolin or guitar. The dimensions for a useful-sized shooting board are given in the illustration.

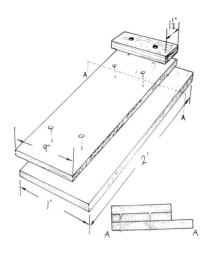

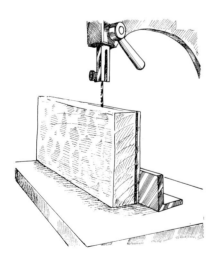

When cuts deeper than that which the saw can accomplish in one pass are needed, make two cuts from opposite sides of the wood and then separate the pieces with a handsaw or a bandsaw.

Machine tools

A small bandsaw and circular saw will save you a lot of time, although they will not be in regular use. If the bandsaw is sharp and set up accurately, you can use it to cut out the neck and scroll, as well as the back and belly of the instrument. It will also cut the thin pieces needed for the sides. A circular saw will save you a lot of time that would otherwise be spent sizing up the timber; it is useful to help true up the joining faces of the back and belly, as well as accurately cutting the sides and the linings.

Adhesive

Hide glue is the only adhesive used in violin making. It is applied hot and makes a weak immediate bond, but dries to give great strength. It is not waterproof. Hot water can be used to separate freshly glued joints and to wash away excess glue. Hide glue becomes weaker after continued reheating, so prepare fresh quantities when required. Twelve hours before the glue is needed, put a small quantity of pearls into a Pyrex bottle and cover them with cold water. The pearls swell as they absorb

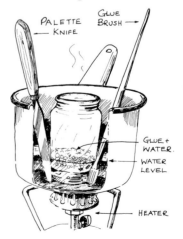

the water. The following day, place the glue bottle in a saucepan of water and heat it. As the temperature rises, the glue liquefies. Add water until the glue runs freely from a brush or knife dipped into and held over the pot. For a weaker bond, add more water. If glue brushes and knives are kept in the outer saucepan, this water will become dilute glue, which is useful for sizing a joint in preparation for glueing.

Sizing entails applying a thinned glue over the surfaces to be joined, and then wiping it away. Follow with the stronger, unthinned glue. This helps to ensure better glue penetration and a stronger joint, and is used in the neck and sometimes when glueing on the end blocks. Details of glueing techniques will be given in the appropriate sections of this book. For applying the glue, use a palette knife, and a small flat, oil colour brush. A second brush kept in the glue water of the outer pan is useful for cleaning away excess glue.

Wood

The illustration shows the parts of a violin. In structure, violas and cellos are much alike. Variations in the choice of woods are often due to the difficulties of finding materials of sufficient size and quality for the larger instruments. The following table lists the components and their woods for a violin; the woods in brackets are some additional woods that would be suitable for use in making a guitar or a mandolin.

Try experimenting with the woods. This is a hobby where the worker who is prepared to experiment will learn quickly. Because some of the skills necessary are quite difficult to learn, it is cheaper and more practical to use un-orthodox woods – the generally accepted woods, if good quality, tend to be very expensive. Make use of homegrown sycamore, pine and spruce. They are virtually indistin-guishable from the best maple and pine that

Which woods to use for different parts of the instrument

Part	Requirements	Wood
Back	This is a thin soundboard. It should be decorative, stiff and resonant	Sycamore, maple, pear, cherry, beech, walnut, willow and ash (rosewood, mahogany)
Sides	These are thin, decorative strips, usually made from the same wood as the back	
Belly	The main sounding board of the instrument. It is thin, stiff and strong, with straight clear grain cut on the quarter	Pine, silver spruce, Western red cedar, hemlock, Douglas fir
Neck	This has to be strong, easy to carve, and hard wearing. It should be decorative	Sycamore, maple, beech (mahogany)
Corner and end blocks	Concealed inside instrument. Straight grain and light weight	Spruce, willow
Linings	Light and straight-grained	Willow, spruce, pine (ash)
Bass bar	Straight-grained pine, often from the same piece as the belly. With cheap instruments, the bass bar may be integral with the belly	

The woods in brackets are suitable for use in guitars and mandolins

comes from Switzerland and Romania. Also, there are the fruitwoods (such as cherry, pear and walnut) and beech, willow, ash and birch, which are all satisfactory for making the back and sides of the instruments. Hemlock, Douglas fir, silver spruce and Western red cedar are all good for the belly of instruments.

To begin using less expensive woods removes some of the stress of working expensive woods with inexperienced hands and the end result will be none the worse. Many of the great instrument makers have used and continue to experiment with woods other than the traditional ones.

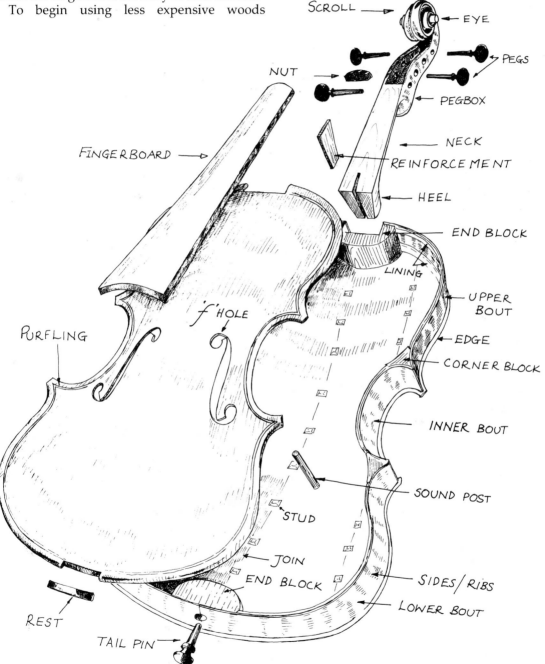

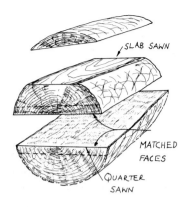

SLAB SAWN

MATCHED
FACES

QUARTER
SAWN

Cutting and storing timber

Most woods used in musical instrument making are sawn on the quarter – that is, when the piece is viewed from the ends, the annual rings stand perpendicular to the sides of the timber. Quarter-sawn timber is stronger, more stable, and easier to work than wood cut on the slab, which has a tendency to warp. In addition, quarter-sawn timber often displays the most attractive figure. When the pieces of the back are taken from adjacent pieces of the same log, and are matched at the glue line in the centre, very beautiful effects can be achieved. You can see that not all the instruments have a symmetrical pattern at the back, the maker having decided that the natural qualities of the wood needed no further organization.

Some of these patterns are produced from planks sawn on the slab, and this is fine for the back and sides. Because the back of the violin is

thin, and the box section structure of the instrument is strong, no serious problems of shrinkage or warping occur, and some delightful grain effects are produced where the timber is lacking in figure.

However, if slab-sawn wood is used for the neck of the instrument, serious problems can occur, particularly if the neck is long and has only the fingerboard glued to the face of the neck to prevent it from twisting off line.

Buying timber

Fruitwoods are not in great demand and the small quantities usually found in country woodyards are often stored in the most inaccessible places. If the wood has been stored for a long time, the ends will split, and will be covered with moss and mould. Once the correct stack has been identified, the direction of the cracks in the ends of the planks will indicate which planks are most nearly sawn on the quarter. Remove these and inspect them carefully. As most logs are slab-sawn, the quarter-sawn timber is likely to rot and crack up the centre.

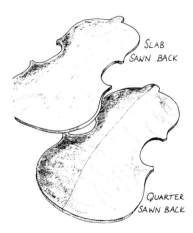

SLAB
SAWN BACK

QUARTER
SAWN BACK

The old heartwood will be no use, but if the rest of the plank is good, make sure that the woodyard does not charge you for the bad part. Inspect the remainder of the wood for knots and splits. Knots are difficult to spot, as they may well be small and intergrown. Sometimes the only evidence of these concealed knots is localized grain distortions, which in sycamore resembles a sporadic figure. Once some likely planks have been chosen, look for rot. Surface darkening, with some blue or black discolouration, indicates the presence of rot. Prod the board with a sharp penknife to reveal soft spots.

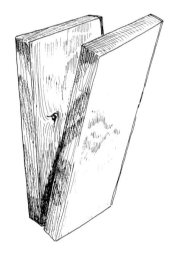

If the plank does not have any spongy areas, then it is probably sound and a valuable addition to the woodstore. Black marks that persist below the surface and are evident after the back or sides of the instruments are carved can usually be bleached out with oxalic acid crystals dissolved in water. Neutralize these with a solution of borax.

Pine and spruce can be bought direct from timber merchants, but some of the best pine for making violin bellies can be found in second-hand furniture warehouses and demolition contractors' yards. Old shelves and floorboards, in particular, provide a rich source of timber, and, although it may not be worthwhile making a special visit to such places, it is worth bearing the prospect in mind when visiting them for other reasons.

Before storing timber, treat all pieces with clear woodworm killer. If wood has been infected by worm, do not immediately discard it, but determine the extent of the damage before using it. Some suggestions for patching infected areas are given on page 60.

Storing timber

Store the timber in a shaded and well ventilated stack. Do not use wood that is inadequately seasoned. As a guide, planks need to stand for a year for every inch of thickness. For violin making, wood should ideally be seasoned for ten or more years before being used, but this is not always practical. Do not use kiln-dried wood.

A month before using wood that has been stored out of doors, bring it inside, and stack it in a warm room. This will lower the moisture content of the wood, and reduce the likelihood of shrinkage once the pieces are cut and fitted.

Part II:

The Violin and Viola

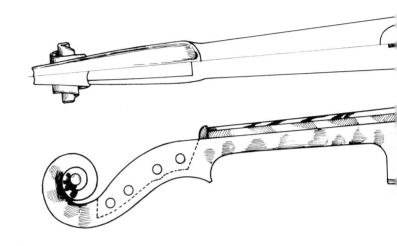

VIOLIN © 1988

No. 1

SCALE:

0   1"   2"   3"

INCHES

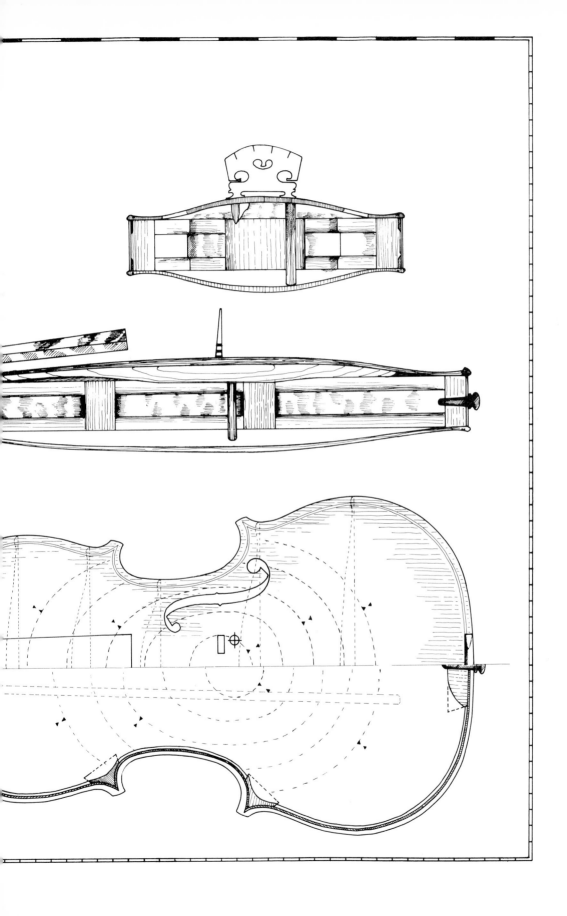

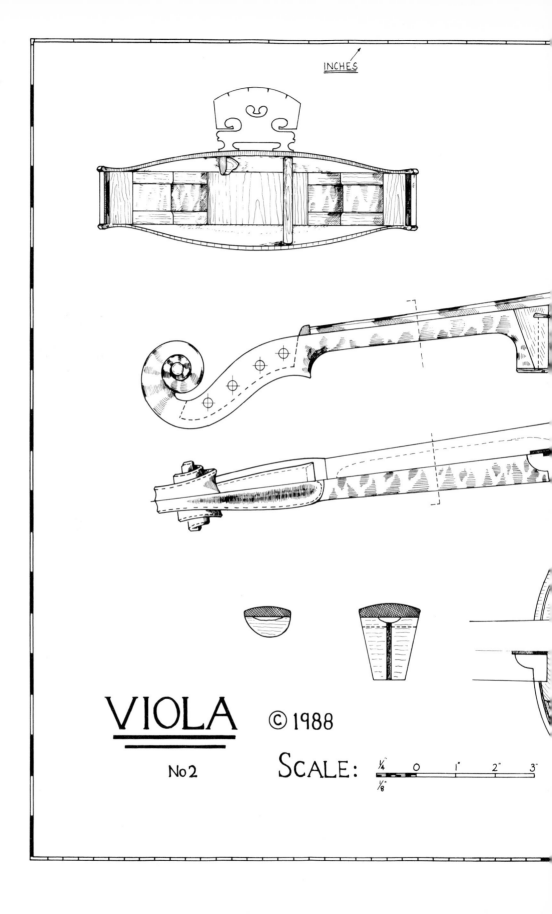

INCHES

VIOLA

© 1988

No 2

SCALE:

¼"
⅛"

0   1"   2"   3"

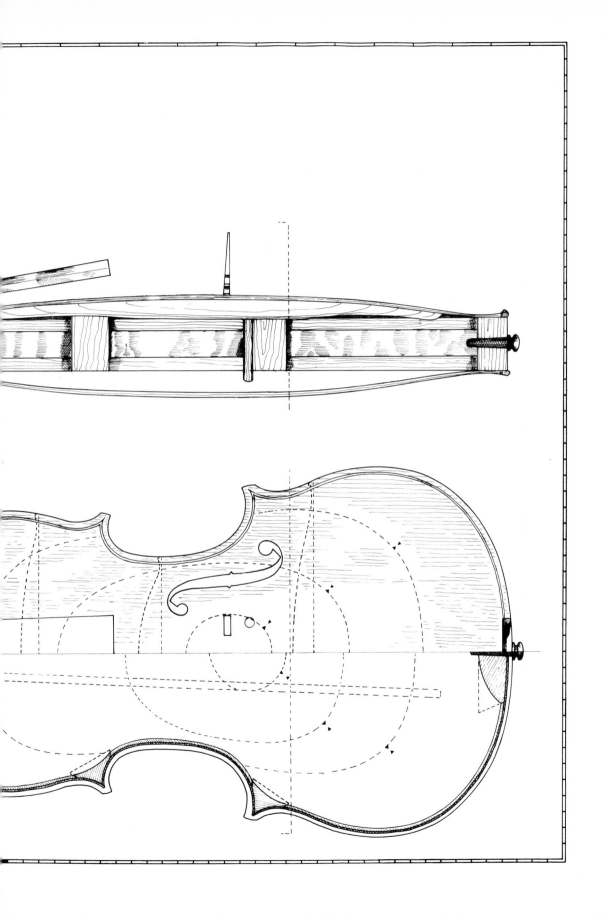

Violin by David Buchanan. Bird's eye maple back and sides.

Violin Viola 'Cello-Construction Sequence

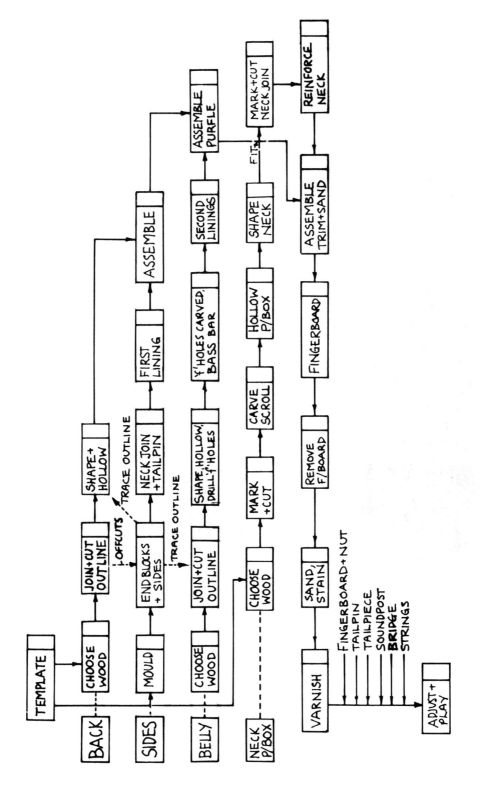

Viola by David Buchanan. Birch back and sides, pine belly.

The Violin and Viola

Designs and materials

Musical instrument making is not only a craft, it is an art. You do not have to be able to draw because the operations in making violins are so leisurely that there is ample time to develop an appreciation of the shapes and to refine these ideas as work progresses.

Do not design the instrument yourself. The shapes are subtle, and the result is unlikely to be better than classical examples which can be copied. Tinker with the detail of the instrument as familiarity with the techniques and shapes grow. Some shapes can be changed slightly, colours and patination can be altered at your whim. You will find that violin making gives you plenty of creative scope.

Study the tracings of the silhouettes, which include a variety of violin shapes – some more attractive than others – and identify the precise differences between them. (See page 71.)

It is a help, when scrutinizing these shapes, to concentrate first on the smaller detail of the instrument, then work towards an appreciation of it as a whole. The scroll and pegbox area is a good place to start, and by looking at the drawings notice that in some instances the scroll and pegbox make a very strong termination to the neck; in others, the lightness of the scroll and the curve of the box which leads to it, give a refinement and delicacy to the instrument.

Study the shape of the 'f' holes and the curve of the bouts, and their relation with each other. In some examples, the outline of the instrument is rather squat, a consequence of the heaviness of the lower bouts, combined with a pinched waist and narrow shoulders. In others, this tendency is less marked, while in some instruments the balance seems perfect.

Choosing a model to copy

We have provided full drawings and moulds of a selection of violins, cellos and violas. Alternatively, choose a handsome instrument and copy it. Using a pencil mounted in the corner of a block of wood, and while keeping the instrument steady with one hand, draw around its outline onto thin cardboard. With the violin on its side, and with the neck held level with the

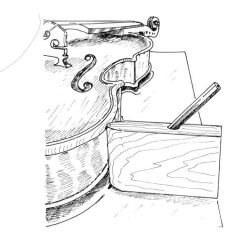

cardboard, draw along its neck and fingerboard and around the scroll and pegbox. This is difficult to do accurately, and it is worthwhile marking the centre of the scroll as you hold the neck against the cardboard. Use dividers to

41

measure off precise dimensions of the pegbox. With the instrument on its side, the arching can be marked off. These, with the width of the sides (which are slightly narrower at the neck of the violin than they are at its base), are the only measurements needed at this stage.

Cut out the profile of the back. Use this as a template to help in selecting wood for the back and belly. Cut around the drawing of the neck; leave additional card at the heel to remind yourself to leave enough extra wood to make it easy to hold the neck while it is being carved.

Choosing the wood

The back
Timber for the back may be selected from wood cut on the quarter or on the slab. If it is cut on the quarter, two matching pieces may be needed to make up the required width. It is easier to fit a single piece back from a slab-sawn log, as these are generally much wider.

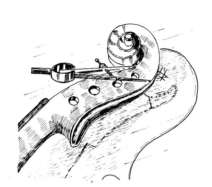

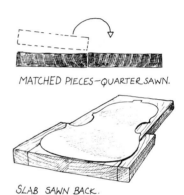

MATCHED PIECES—QUARTER SAWN.

SLAB SAWN BACK.

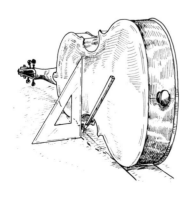

Whichever board you choose, look closely at its outer edges to ensure that the template does not encroach on the sapwood of the log. Sapwood is usually easy to identify, as it is paler, and softer, and has a wider grain pattern than the heartwood. If the wood is particularly beautiful, and not quite large enough, small pieces can be glued to the sides. This method is described on the next page.

When you have chosen your timber, mark the outline of the template onto the wood, leaving an adequate allowance for shooting the join. Inspect the area enclosed by the line for knots, splits and other defects. If, after very close scrutiny and perhaps some adjustment to the position of the template, the piece selected seems good in all respects, cut it to length, and test it for soundness. Lift the wood as illustrated, balancing it between the thumb and

edges and the face side as illustrated. Level each face side. For a violin, the slabs of wood can be held in the vice; with larger instruments, they will have to be placed and planed on a flat surface. Run the plane lengthwise down the board and then finish each piece with diagonal passes to level the corners and middle. Any major twist in the surface can be detected by using two winding sticks (illustrated below).

Place one board, edge up, in the vice. Use a set square to assess the extent to which the edge is off-square to the face side. Set the block plane to a fine cut and, using it as illustrated, weave it

first finger of the right hand, and hold it to your ear. Tap the wood with the other hand. A sound board resonates clearly. Wood that is cracked buzzes as it is struck, and rotten wood resonates dully. The sound given by the board should be clear. If it isn't, check it carefully for faults, as it is better to stop and change pieces at this stage than to wait until later.

The belly
Choose two pieces of quarter-sawn pine or spruce for the belly. These should be matched for similarities of grain and, if possible, taken from the same piece of wood. The grain must be clean and straight from top to bottom of the instrument. Cut them to length and test them for resonance as described above.

Joining the back and belly

Violin makers are often judged by their skill in making the joint down the centre of the back. Unlike the joint in the belly, this is a long exposed joint, in a wood that is so uniform that a black glueline running straight down the middle can seriously blemish the instrument's appearance. Take each piece, mark the jointing

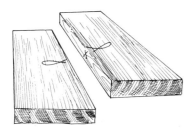

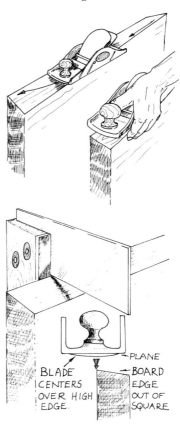

BLADE CENTERS OVER HIGH EDGE.

PLANE

BOARD EDGE OUT OF SQUARE

down the surface of the edge to true it. Repeat for the other side.

Once the second edge is squared, place the first upon it, face sides facing outwards, and inspect the joint. If the edge has been perfectly trued, both boards should stand in the same vertical plane. If they don't, correct them before using a straightedge to identify longtitudinal faults in the joint. Ease down the high spots with a block plane.

When the joint is almost perfect, rub flake white powder over the jointing edge of the part not held in the vice. Rub the planks together, limiting the longitudinal movement to 1 inch. Set the block plane to the finest cut, and plane away the high spots revealed by the chalk marks left on the edge. Repeat, taking finer cuts each time, until they fit perfectly. Leave them together with their ends aligned and draw a pencil line or two across the joint. This will help locate the position when glueing.

Take the two pieces of pine for the belly. The grain should run straight and parallel with the sides of each board. Inspect the end grain in order to identify the edges which were closest to the centre of the trunk. The curvature of the annual rings, which form concentric rings centred on the heartwood, will probably make identification easy, but if the board was cut from a large tree and the curvature of the annual rings is not obvious, inspect the individual ring markings. Each dark line represents a summer's growth. The pale growth between the lines is the lightweight vigorous spring growth. As the spring turns to summer, growth slows and the wood shades darken slightly to merge with the summer growth. The centre of the tree is towards the side where the light spring growth is juxtaposed with the sharply contrasting dark summer growth of the year before.

Position the finer grained heartwood at the centre of the belly, and mark the edges to be joined.

Use the procedure described above for shooting the joint in the belly. Heat the hide glue and warm the edges of the boards. Do not remove the residue of white from the edge as this will help to whiten the glue and disguise the joint.

Glueing the back and belly

Lay the bar clamps on the workbench and adjust them to the width of the back. Brush glue quickly onto both edges of the back, press them together and rub them in a longitudinal direction, increasing hand pressure as you do

so. Stop, with the pencil lines aligned, as soon as the joint tightens. Place the back between the jaws of the bar clamp and, with padding pieces in place, tighten slowly. Do not tighten the clamps fully until the C-clamps are in place, holding the battens across the joint as illustrated. Repeat with the belly.

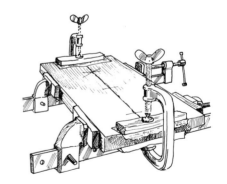

The sides

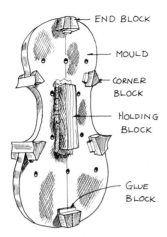

END BLOCK

MOULD

CORNER BLOCK

HOLDING BLOCK

GLUE BLOCK.

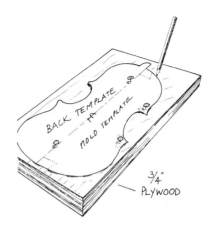

The violin sides are shaped around a mould. Some suppliers will supply moulds with corner and end blocks already cut and ready for shaping, with the plans of their range of instruments. For a small additional fee, they will cut a mould from a cardboard template supplied by the maker. However, for those wanting to make their own mould, the procedures are straightforward.

Fold the cardboard template in half, down its centreline. One half will be recut to the shape of the mould, while the other remains true to the final outline of the instrument.

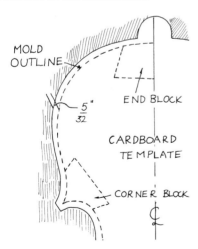

MOLD OUTLINE

$\frac{5}{32}$"

END BLOCK

CARDBOARD TEMPLATE

CORNER BLOCK

On the left side of the template, mark in a line $5/32$ in from the outside edge. Follow this line across the top of the template, cutting off the button. Prick in the position of the corner and end blocks as illustrated. These are made from straight-grained spruce, in the section of a truncated triangle. Mark in the positions for the blocks and then cut around the half mould profile.

Fix the template with two drawing pins through the centreline to some $3/4$ in plywood or chipboard and draw around the mould template. Using the same pin holes, reverse the template and draw around the other side. Using the pin holes as a guide, mark a centre-line down the mould, square round the ends and mark the line down the opposite side.

Cut out the template with a bandsaw, taking care to keep the cut clean and regular. Cut out the slots for the blocks. Drill some $1/4$ in holes in the positions indicated for short lengths of dowel to anchor elastic bands, holding the ribs in position while they are being glued.

Setting up the mould

Select straight-grained wood for the corner and end blocks. Four corner blocks and two end blocks are needed. Plane them until they slide easily into the dovetailed notches in the mould.

Cut the corner and end blocks to length. They should all be the same length, equal to the maximum side width at the bottom of the instrument.

Arrange some temporary packing pieces to lift the mould off the surface of the table by about $1/4$ in and drop the corner and end blocks

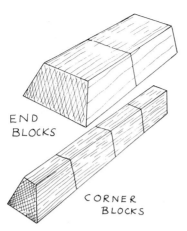

END
BLOCKS

CORNER
BLOCKS

side of the mould a wooden block; this should protrude slightly from the surface level of the end and corner blocks. The wooden block can be tacked, screwed or glued on; if you use glue, place newspaper between the glueing faces so that you can unfix them later. With the blocks attached, the mould can be held in a carpenter's vice as you work on the sides.

Shaping the mould

With a straightedge, lightly mark the centreline of the mould onto the end blocks. Using this as a guide, pin the mould template over the end

into position. Check that they are vertical, using a set square or filing card. Slip a small glue block onto the mould and behind each block and leave the glue to chill.

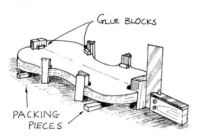

GLUE BLOCKS

PACKING
PIECES

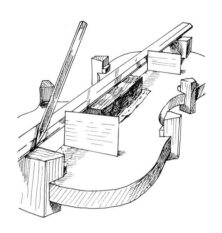

Turn the mould over and repeat on the other side, always taking care to avoid dribbling glue between the blocks and the mould. Leave the mould until the glue has set and the corner and end blocks are firmly fixed into position.

From workshop scraps, cut and fix to each

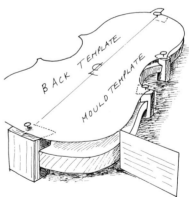

BACK TEMPLATE

MOULD TEMPLATE

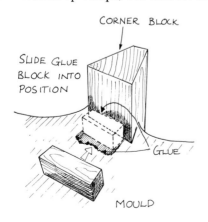

CORNER BLOCK

SLIDE GLUE
BLOCK INTO
POSITION

GLUE

MOULD

and corner blocks. Use a set square or a filing card to check that the line of the template conforms with the outside curves of the mould and move the template until it does. Fasten the template securely and draw around it, marking the line for the sides onto the end grain of the

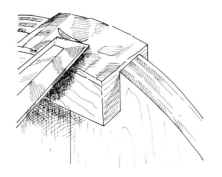

blocks. Reverse the template to complete the marking in on the first side.

Remove the template and place the mould upright in the vice. Pare away surplus wood on the end block with a sharp chisel, until it is almost level with the pencil line. Repeat this at the other end, taking care to ensure that the mould and blocks form a regular and gentle curve. This can be tested by bending a steel hacksaw blade or thin steel straightedge around the edge of the mould.

Remove the mould from the vice and lay it flat on the bench. Check the verticality of the end blocks and adjust these with a chisel before finishing off and smoothing with a rough file.

Using the end blocks as additional reference points, fit the template to the reverse side of the mould and draw in the lines on the corner blocks.

Shape the corner blocks in exactly the same way, finishing with gouge and files. With marks at each end of the block, it is always possible to work with the grain. Ensure that the curves

follow the sweeps of the mould and, before finishing each corner block, use a filing card or set square to check its verticality. The finished mould should resemble the illustration on page 45.

Cutting the sides of the violin

The sides are usually cut from wood sawn from the back board. Remove surplus glue from its face side and plane it flat as described on page 43. With a marking gauge or a pencil held between thumb and forefinger (with the second finger used as a fence), draw a line ¼ in in from its edge. This is a cutting line and does not represent the finished thickness at the back.

Place the back upright in the vice. Cut off two wedges with a ripsaw, using the centre join and the line drawn around the edge as a guide. This cut usually takes a long time. Do not hurry or press the saw into the cut, or the blade will wander off line. When both wedges have been removed, trim them to their approximate width with a backsaw. Make an identifying mark at the end of each wedge to show which side of the back it has been taken from. Level the freshly sawn faces with a shoulder plane, resting the offcut on a sloping shooting board held in the vice.

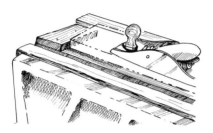

Once their face sides have been smoothed, mark a new 1/16 in cutting line and saw off a side strip from each piece with a circular saw or rip saw, with a plank clamped against the board to prevent the side strip from snapping. You will need more wood than can be obtained from a single strip the length of the back, so once the first side strips are cut from the wedges, smooth the face side of the remaining waste pieces and saw off a second strip from each side. Mark them as before.

Trimming the side strips to size

Use an offcut of straight pine as a width guide fitted to the shooting board. Select a side strip and tack the guide parallel to the edge of the board, slightly further in than the finished side width.

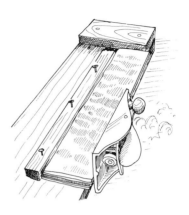

Place the strips on the shooting board. Press them against the edge support and trim the overhanging edges with the block plane. Stop planing when the sole of the plane touches the side of the shooting board. Alter the position of the support strips, setting it to the maximum side width, and trim the strips' second edge.

Smoothing the sides

Preliminary smoothing is done with the block plane set to a fine cut. If the wood is decorative, it may be necessary to hone the blade to a steeper sharpening angle, as described on page 17.

Select some cardboard or thick veneer and spray mount them with aerosol adhesive to the surface of a smooth pine board, with just sufficient space between them for a side strip. Hold the end of the strip closest to you with a C-clamp, and plane down the side strip surface. With the plane set to a fine cut, it should be possible to smooth away all saw marks. Finish with scrapers, a razor blade, and then fine sandpaper. Turn the strip over and work it down to the level of the cards. Exchange the edging strips as they become bruised and abraded.

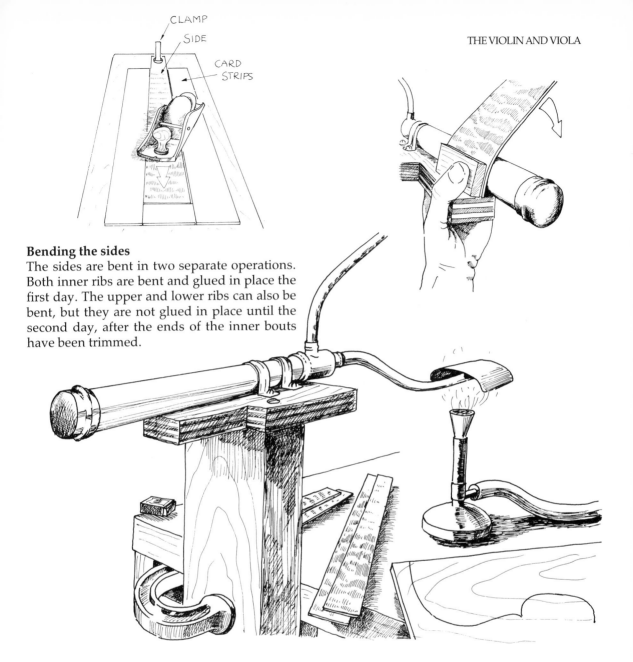

CLAMP
SIDE
CARD STRIPS

Bending the sides

The sides are bent in two separate operations. Both inner ribs are bent and glued in place the first day. The upper and lower ribs can also be bent, but they are not glued in place until the second day, after the ends of the inner bouts have been trimmed.

Clamp the bending iron to the side of the bench, with its boiling end 2 in above the top of the gas burner. Make sure that there is approximately half a cupful of water in the bending iron. Light the burner and leave the iron to warm up. Keep some spare strips nearby for practising.

Place the mould, side uppermost, in the vice. Place the mould template over some scrap wood and draw around its profile; keep this handy as a reference when bending the sides.

Square off the ends of the side strips, cutting away any cracks or suspect timber. Store the sides in pairs, according to which side of the back they were originally sawn from. Arrange their face sides so that they are matching and mark them.

As soon as the vent pipe is steaming, loosely fit the end plug to inhibit the loss of water.

49

Experiment with a spare scrap of side strip before commencing to bend the side strips. Select a side strip and hold it against the bending iron. As the wood heats up, it will become slightly pliable. As soon as the wood is really hot, slowly and firmly bend it into shape.

Make frequent references to the outline of the bouts marked on the scrap wood to check that the size and shape are being followed.

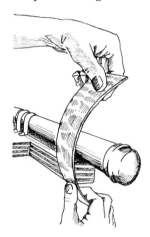

On the curves with a greater radius, move the strip slowly over the pipe. Press firmly and make sure that you are not introducing local distortions. It is easier to bend the wood than it is to straighten out a curve once it has been bent over the hot pipe.

If the bending iron is too cool or the worker tries to bend the wood too quickly, the wood will break. In contrast to new wood, old dry wood is difficult to bend, and so is wood that is highly figured, as its grain is very short. If the wood is particularly difficult to bend, cut a strip

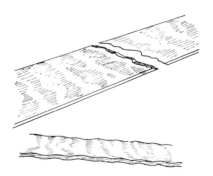

of thin flexible tin from the side of an engine oil can; this should be as wide as the sides and 2 in longer than the longest strip that has to be bent. Wrap the ends of the tin smartly round the ends of the side strip, and with the tin on the outside of the curve and while gripping the tin against the ends of the strip, slowly ease the side strip into its required curve. The tin strip prevents the outer fibres of the side strip from tearing out as they stretch and also keeps the strip hotter.

Work the curve and check continually the overall shape of the piece. Pay particular attention to the points where the sides are glued to the corner blocks. These must be a perfect fit, as it is difficult to apply sufficient clamping pressure to force the side into position.

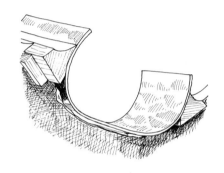

Once the strip fits neatly into the mould, cut it to length, leaving about ¼ in surplus at each end. Take a strip for the opposite side, and after ensuring that the grain on the face sides match, bend this into the opposite bout.

Before glueing these two pieces, bend the other strips into their required shapes and leave them for the next day.

Glueing the inner bouts

Once bent, the inner ribs should fit the mould and rest snugly against the corner blocks, with enough spring to hold them in position. With the mould in the vice, side uppermost, remove the inner rib and cut a thin strip of newspaper to lie against the mould between the corner blocks. While the glue is heating, collect some thick rubber bands and some small wooden

dowels and strips of varied section to hold the side in place. With the short ¼ in dowels inserted in the mould to anchor the bands, experiment with various methods of springing the rib and holding it in place using the rubber bands to give the necessary tension.

As soon as the glue is hot, clamp the middle of the side in place with some rubber bands; then, tackling the ends in turn, dip a glue knife into the hot glue, spring out the end of the side and slip the knife between the corner block and the side. Run the glue quickly onto the corner block, wipe the knife on the side and press the side to the corner block. A little glue should ooze from the joint. If a lot comes out, too much was applied, and later the mould will have to be released with care at that corner, as the glue may have run between the side and the mould. If no glue seeps from the joint, it might indicate that it has chilled before the joint was

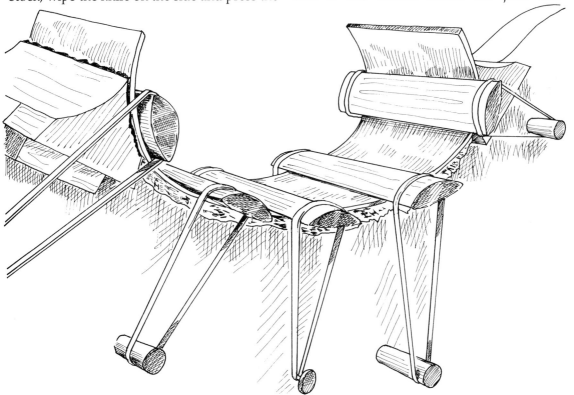

assembled. Open the join, and clean it with a warm damp brush. Reglue it with more speed, in a higher workshop temperature, and perhaps use thinner glue.

Arrange some dowels and wood pads to hold the joint, making them fast with rubber bands, and repeat at the other end of the bout. Turn the mould so that its other side is uppermost, and glue the opposite rib.

Trimming the inner ribs
Leave the glue to set for about 12 hours at room temperature. Mark off the cutting line for the

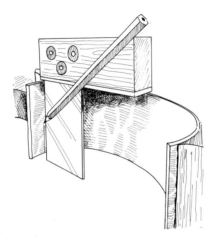

bout with a set square. Because the sides are scarfed at the corners, the cutting line should be about ⅛ in above the apex of the corner block.

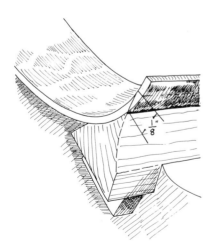

Mark this line in pencil and sight down the side to check that the line is square with the edge of the mould. Adjust if necessary and cut the strip off with a sharp knife. Repeat at the other three corners, each time checking the alignment of the ends.

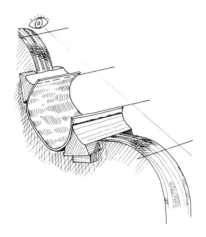

With a sharp gouge, trim the edge of the side until its inner edge follows the exact curve of the corner block. Hold a block of wood against the side while it is pared away. Smooth out irregularities with sandpaper backed onto a curved block. Repeat at the other three corners.

Fitting the upper and lower ribs
Take the side strip marked for the top rib, fit it into the corner block and check its fit. The curve at the corner block should fit snugly into the block and tight against the tip of the inner bout. If the radius is too small, slight adjustments can be made while the wood is cold, but if more of

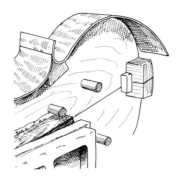

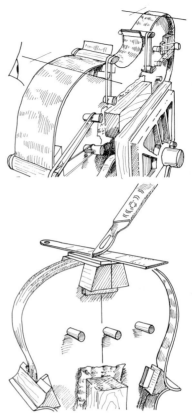

a bend is required, the bending iron will have to be used.

Once the end at the corner block is fitted, clamp it in place with pads and rubber bands, and mark and trim the other end. This need not extend to the centreline, as the slot for the neck is cut at this point. Trim the side just short of the centreline. Repeat for the other side and then fit the strip for the lower bout on the first side. This is done exactly as for the top bout, except that the side should be trimmed to overlap the centreline at the bottom block.

With newspaper strips interposed between the mould and sides, glue the two top bouts and the lower bout. In each case they should be held in position with pads and rubber bands and checked for squareness with the sides of the mould.

Spring up the side at the corner block, insert glue as before, taking care not to run it onto the mould. Glue the sides at the end blocks once the corner blocks are glued and clamp them with bands and pads.

The last rib is fitted after the others have been

left to dry. Turn the mould to sit in the vice, bottom block uppermost, and square off the centreline. Cut this with a knife and lift off the waste. The last side is fitted at the bottom block first. Take care that the join down the centreline is square, and that the join at the corner block is good. The latitude for adjustment once this side has been cut is small, all of it being at the corner

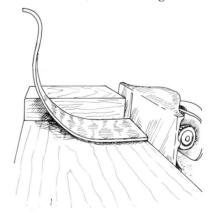

block. Very fine and accurate shavings can be removed from the ends of the rib by resting the strip across a simple shooting board and slicing off the end with the block plane as illustrated.

Glue the side at the end block first, clamp it with pads and then glue the corner block. For a decorative effect, insert a slither of black mounting paper or a strip of inlay into the joint at the bottom block before you slide the side into position. When it is cleaned up, the inlay will enhance the appearance of the joint.

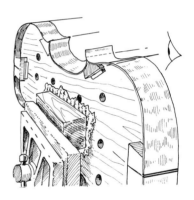

Trimming the corners
The corners must be trimmed in pairs to ensure that they are in line with each other.

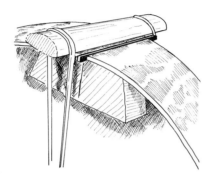

INNER BOUT

Turn the mould on its side. Look at each corner block in turn and mark on the newly fastened ribs where the inner bout terminates. Mark at both edges and lightly square across with a ruler. Sight down the sides to check the alignment of the corners and the sides, and correct them if necessary. If they are badly out, one of the bouts is twisted. This should have been spotted earlier, but you can amend it: unglue the twisted section by working the joint apart with a hot knife and refasten it.

Once the line for the corners is established, rest a small straightedge or old hacksaw blade against the line and cut off the surplus with a knife. The cut should be just beyond the joint between the two sides. Lightly file the edge to remove roughness, but do not round its corners. Use this corner as an additional reference when marking out the second corner on this side, which is marked and cut in precisely the same way as described above. Repeat this procedure on the other side so that all four corners are trimmed and square.

Levelling the sides
Remove the mould-holding blocks or make a recess in a flat board to allow the mould to lie flat. Take the block plane, and adjust it to a very fine cut. With the mould lying face down on the board, and with the end block resting against a stop, run the plane around its edge. Do not worry about splitting the inside edges of the corner and end blocks. At this stage there is ample waste wood which has to be trimmed away once the mould is removed.

The sides must be level and can be checked after trimming by inverting the mould over the board. Small irregularities over a distance of about 3 in are not significant, and although the violin will be better if all lines are straight and

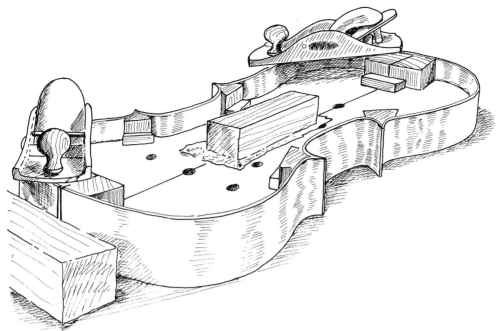

and true, the back and belly will twist and bend to accommodate slight inaccuracies. End and corner blocks and the sides adjacent to them must all be on the same plane.

Pencil 'belly' on the face of the mould on the side that has been levelled, and turn the mould so that the other sides can be trimmed.

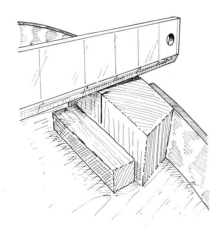

Because the instrument tapers slightly towards the neck, more wood will have to be removed from this side. Mark up at the end blocks the heights of the sides, using the levelled face as a reference. Rest the mould, belly downwards on a board, and lodge a pair of pencils or short dowels beneath the mould at the inner bouts, to lift the mould and allow it to rock slightly. Arrange shims of cardboard beneath the ends of the instrument, until both height marks are an equal distance above the board. Stabilize the mould to prevent it moving, and then add a few weights to the top of the belly to hold it steady.

Using a filing card marked to the height at the ends, draw round the sides, marking off the taper. Cut round the sides, close to the line, with a scalpel resting against a flexible steel hacksaw blade. Saw away the prominent ends of the blocks, and then plane the sides down as described for the first side.

UPPER BOUT   LOWER BOUT

Cutting the slot for the neck
Cut the slot for the neck while the sides and
blocks are held by the mould.

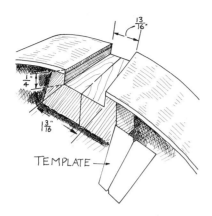

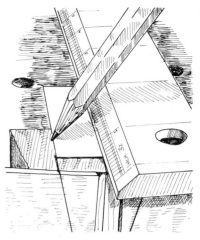

The dimensions for the tapered slot are given
in the above illustration. Those for the cello and
the viola, can be taken from the plans on
pages 131-2 and 37-8, respectively. Using the
dimensions, mark and cut out a cardboard
template. With the mould sitting upright in the
vice, align the template with the centrelines
marked on the end of the neck end block. Draw
down both sides.

centre of the mould, to mark in the sides of the
slot. Invert the mould and mark in the slot base
line and sides.

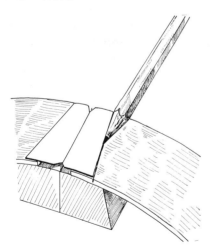

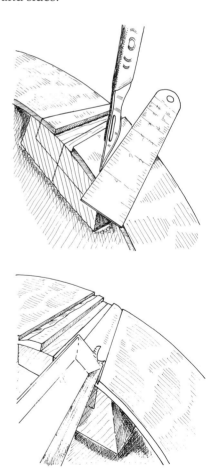

Place the mould face up on the bench and
measure in ¼ in from the edge down the
centreline. Square across the baseline for the
slot. Use a slip of filing card cut for the purpose,
resting it against a straightedge lined on the

Check these thoroughly before replacing the mould in the vice. Place a straightedge against the line for one side of the slot and cut down it. Use a chisel to relieve the waste side of the line, and then saw down to the base line with the backsaw. Repeat on the other side. Chisel away the waste until the recess reaches the baseline at both sides. Check that the base of the slot is level and remark the centrelines in the slot.

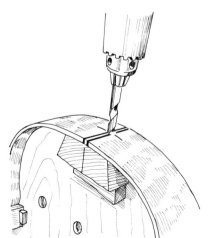

Drilling the hole for the end pin

Invert the mould in the vice, and at the centre-point of the join at the bottom of the instrument drill a ¼ in hole through the sides and end block. Use a brad-point drill if one is available as it is easier to control than a metalwork drill and

less liable to tear up the grain. Ream the hole when the instrument is assembled.

Linings

Linings serve to increase the glued surface area at the edge of the sides. They are made from very thin strips of spruce, pine or willow. Other woods easier to bend, such as ash, can be used, but they are heavy and not as good as the lighter woods.

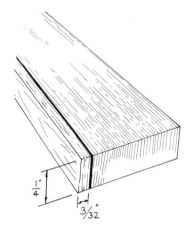

Select an offcut of pine or spruce which has close, straight grain. The annual rings should lie exactly parallel to the side of the board. Saw or plane the board until it is ¼ in thick, and plane the outside edge, adjusting the angle of the edge to run true with the grain. Then, with a backsaw or circular saw, cut off the first lining strip ¹⁄₁₆ in thick. Plane away the saw marks on

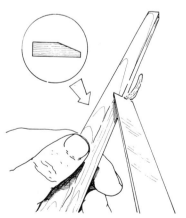

the lining strip and work a bevel on the sawn side with a sharp chisel.

Plane up the new edge to the board and cut off another lining strip; repeat until there are sufficient strips for both faces of the mould. Cut some spare in case they are needed.

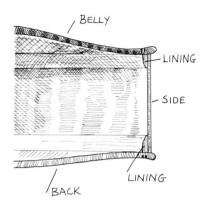

The linings are glued all round the inside edge of the instrument, but at this point only one set can be fitted, otherwise it would be impossible to remove the mould. The bevel removes unnecessary wood and keeps the interior of the instrument free from unwelcome hard edges. Also, by graduating the reinforcement piece, the bevel eliminates a hard spot which would become a stress point in the construction. Each lining terminates at a corner or end block, which is dovetailed into the mould. Because of the taper of these blocks, the end of the linings can be cut at an angle, and slipped into the tapered space between the block and the side.

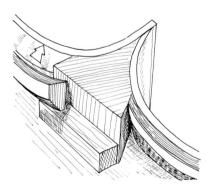

Fitting the linings

Before the linings are glued in place, remove the small glue blocks holding the corner and end blocks with a small chisel and a light mallet.

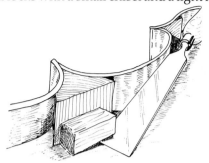

Place the mould face down on the table. Place the edge of the chisel between the mould and the block and give the chisel a smart tap. Once the glue blocks on both sides are removed, lightly tap the mould until it frees itself from any stray glue that may have trickled between the sides and the mould. If this proves difficult, it may be necessary to slip a warmed glue knife between the sides and the mould and pry them apart. Once the mould is free, return it to its original position and warm up the glue.

Assemble the assortment of lining clamps illustrated on page 24. Fit the linings to the edge of the sides which are glued to the back first, starting by fitting the linings to the upper and lower bouts. Taper the end of the lining strip so that it fits exactly into the small crevice between the corner block and the side, and then dip the tip of the lining in the hot glue water. After a

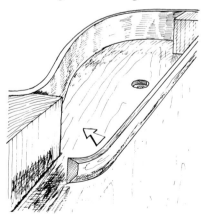

minute, remove the strip, and bend it against the side of the glue pot, or any other warm rounded shape. Only a small curve is required, the rest of the strip can be bent cold into position. As soon as the end fits snugly into the corner block, spring the lining into place, marking with a knife the position and angle for the cut at the end block. Remove the lining, cut it, replace it and leave it there until all the linings have been fitted on the first side.

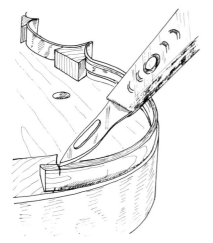

The linings for the inner bouts are more difficult to fit and keep in position, because they spring away from the side they are supposed to support. Fit these with great care, and do not cut them to length until the bending is accomplished at both ends and you are confident that they will fit.

Glueing the linings

Take great care not to allow surplus glue to slip between the sides and the mould. Use a thin mixture and test it by dipping the brush into the glue. When the glue is hot it should flow readily off the tip of the brush with the consistency of cream. Glue the upper and lower bout linings first. Remove the first lining, brush hot glue onto its glueing surface, wipe off, apply some more, and then slip the lining into its position, easing it down until it is level with the sides. Never push it down below this level. Fit the clamps around the lining at very close intervals. If in some places the glue appears to have chilled before a satisfactory join was made,

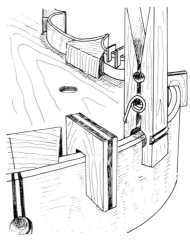

warm the glue knife and run a little more glue into the join. Repeat all round the instrument. When all of the linings have been fitted to the first side, place several thin slips of side offcuts under the mould and then press the mould smartly downwards to separate it from glue that may have run between the mould and the sides. Leave the mould until the glue has hardened, and then trim the linings flush with the sides.

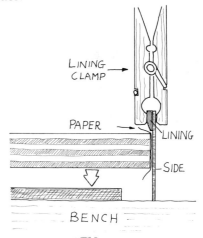

The back

Take the back slab and place it, flat face up, on the workbench. Take the mould that still has the sides fixed to it and place it on top of the back. Align the centreline of the mould with the join down the middle of the back and check

round the sides to see if there is sufficient room
for the small overhang between the sides and
the back. Unless something went very wrong
with the work on the sides, there should be
ample room; if there isn't, glue some small and
inconspicuous pieces to the edge of the back.

When selecting suitable offcuts, hold the
back and the offcuts to the light. Vary the
direction of the light and the viewpoint.
Although they may seem alike when seen flat
on, their reflective qualities may be startlingly
different when viewed at an angle. Especially
when matching wood as iridescent as
sycamore, it is often the similarities in the
reflective properties rather than the grain
patterns which should be given priority. Join
the additional pieces to the back the same way
as the centreline was joined. Plane up the face
side before drawing the complete outline of the
sides on the back.

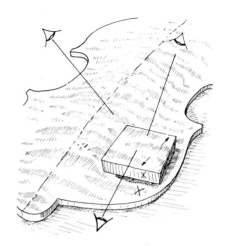

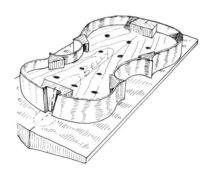

Patching wormholes

It sometimes happens that the saw or gouge
reveals a small blemish, such as a wormhole or
knot. Provided that they are no larger than
$\frac{1}{2} \times \frac{1}{2}$ in it is often better to patch the wood
than to discard it. This saves the wood and the
effort that has already gone into shaping it, and
it also gives you an opportunity to enhance the
wood by inserting a well-fitted patch.

Establish the extent of the blemish and select
a piece of wood that can be used for the patch.
Both the grain and the figure should match and,
when selecting the piece, remember to check it
from all angles to ensure that its reflective
qualities are compatible with the area in which
you insert it. Selecting the right piece,

particularly for the back, is the most time-
consuming part of this job, but well worth it
and preferable to disguising a bad match.

Having chosen the piece, mark on it its
orientation in relation to the back of the violin.
Take a small piece of filing card or a self-
adhesive label, and sketch in the patch outline.
It should have straight sides – the best shapes
are a diamond or a square, but whichever shape
is chosen, ensure that the chisel can clean out
the corners without difficulty. Mark on the
template the orientation of the top and bottom
of the instrument, and then glue it in its correct
orientation to the part of the offcut designated
for the patch.

Cut this out with a backsaw and under-cut its
edges with a chisel or a block plane.

Peel off the paper template and place the
patch over the blemish. Align it correctly and

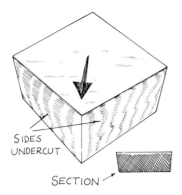

SIDES
UNDERCUT

SECTION

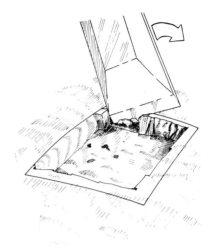

tack it in place with a drop of cyanoacrilate glue once its position is established.

As soon as the glue has set, take a sharp knife or scalpel and, with firm pressure, mark once round the edge of the patch. Slip a knife beneath the patch to remove it. With a ¼ in bevel-edged chisel and a light mallet, chip out the wood inside the lines defining the patch. Never stray closer than ¹⁄₁₆ in to the line. Excavate the full depth of the patch and level its floor before trimming around the edge in the following way.

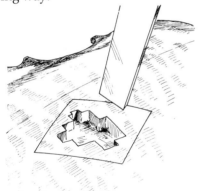

Lodge the blade of the chisel in the knife-cut at the centre of one side. Press downwards, with the chisel angled slightly to match the slope at the edges of the patch. Do the same at each side. Change to a slightly larger chisel, strop it and lodge it in the cut, with the remaining edge hovering over the knife-cut. Use a guillotine motion to cut the remaining part of each side. With care, a perfect cut should result. Repeat this at each side, paying

particular attention to the corners, which must be thoroughly cleaned out. Check that the patch fits by holding it over the recess, then lightly bevel its underedges.

Take a small quantity of hide glue and heat it. When the glue is ready, stir in a few grains of flake white powder to the liquid glue. Apply the lightened glue to the edge of the patch, and to the sides and bottom of the hole. Insert the patch and tap it firmly into position with a hammer, using a woodpad to spread the load.

Cutting the back

With the mould resting on the face side of the back slab, align the centrelines and adjust the mould longitudinally to allow room for the button at the top of the back. Hold the mould tightly with one hand and draw around the

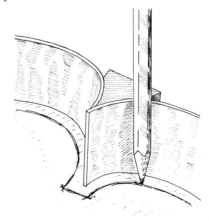

sides with the other. If the pencil is held vertically and pressed against the sides, the outline will be accurate. Remember to include wood for the top button when marking and cutting out the back. Check once more, with the back template, adding more at the corners if necessary, before cutting around the edge with a coping saw or bandsaw.

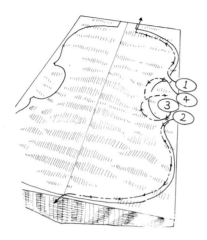

Whether cutting by hand or with a bandsaw, there is an order for cutting the outline of the instrument which helps to eliminate the possibility of splitting off some of the short grain timber at the corners. The order is the same for the belly, where the softwood is even more inclined to split along the grain than the sycamore or fruitwoods. The illustration shows the order for cutting. The corners of the instrument are the most vulnerable, so the cuts all start at the corners and clear the danger area as quickly as possible. Start by sawing off the top bouts, then the lower bouts. Finish by cutting the line of the inner bouts. Each centre bout requires two cuts, which meet in the middle.

If a bandsaw is used, the angles of the back will make accurate cutting difficult. A simple block clamped to the bandsaw table, raising the face of the table at the blade, helps to enable the operator to support the back level while sawing.

The last sawing job on the back is to remove from the top and bottom of the slab two large wedges.

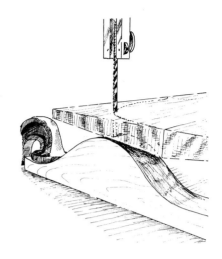

Draw a line around the edge of the upper and lower bouts ¼ in in from the face side. Use this as a sawing guide. Hold the slab, bottom up, in the vice, and saw away all but the smallest slither joining the wedge to the main piece. Invert the back and saw off the top wedge. Then cut free the remaining wedge at the bottom, this having served to hold the slab while the top wedge was cut.

The slab should now resemble the back of the violin, its flat surfaces suggesting the smooth curves that remain to be carved. With the homemade gauge illustrated on page 24 resting against the face side of the back slab, scribe a line around the edge. This line establishes the thickness ($^5/_{32}$ in) of the back at its outer edge.

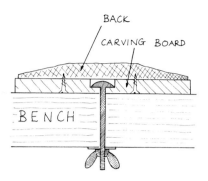

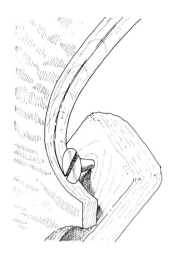

Preparation for carving the back

In order to be carved, the back must be held firmly. One good way of holding it is to fix it to a board pivoted to the bench.

Take a flat board, a little larger than the violin back, and a long coach bolt with a washer and a wing nut. Drill a shank hold for the bolt in the centre of the board and another in the top of the workbench. Carve a depression around the lip of the hole to countersink the head. Invert the board and drill and countersink two holes for the screws close to the bolt hole. Choose two wood screws long enough to pass through the board into the back, but short enough not to penetrate beyond the waste wood, which will be carved from the inside of the back.

With the bolt in place, position the board over the back, and, starting the screws with a bradawl, screw the board to the back. Poke the bolt through the hole in the bench, slip on the washer and wingnut, and tighten. The back is thus securely mounted, and by releasing the wingnut, it can be rotated to suit the needs of the carver.

Rough shaping

Set up the angled lamp to give a low light. With much of the wood removed already, the

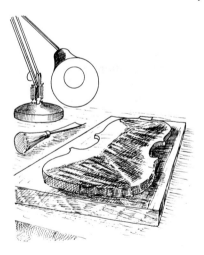

prospect of carving the back may still seem daunting. Working at a gentle pace, rough shaping should not take more than two or three hours, yet this is one of the more artistically demanding aspects of the whole process as the major shapes, which express your preference, are determined at this stage.

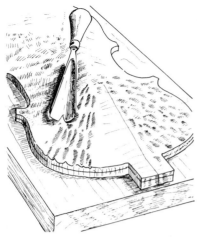

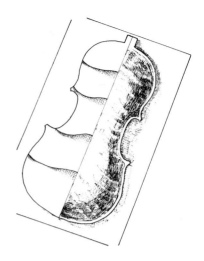

Take the large gouge and carve away the corners between the cuts on the back. Try to introduce additional planes to the surface of the back. Continually check the symmetry of the carving by sighting down the back from a low angle. Carve the edges close to the scribed line.

It is important not only to check the longitudinal symmetry of the instrument, but also to sight across the instrument. The back should curve gracefully from end to end, the highest point close to the inner bouts.

SECTIONS THROUGH BACK.

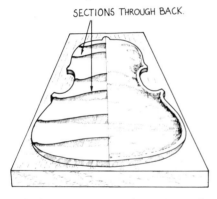

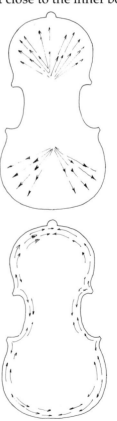

Although this is a matter of artistic preference, it is a good idea to limit the depression at the sides to the area over and immediately adjacent to the purfling, which is only about ³⁄₁₆ in from the edge. By extending a concavity towards the centre of the instrument, there is a danger that the back of the instrument will look pinched and hungry.

Work quickly and concentrate on each cut. Never try to remove more wood in one pass than can be easily managed, and make sure that each cut completely removes its own shaving, leaving the wood cleaner and shapelier as a result.

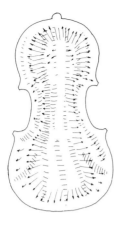

The illustrations show the steps in carving the back. Once the edge around the back has been levelled, do not cut below the edge line at the purfling. The final depression here will be sunk once the purfling is in place. Bring the sides up from the edge in a gentle curve once the purfling line is passed. Before long, the major shaping will have been accomplished and after a thorough check, level the irregularities in the carved surface. Focus the angle lamp on the work, take a flat gouge and, working downwards and from the edge, remove the larger irregularities. This leaves smaller ripples to be levelled. During this meticulous operation look for faults and asymmetries in the back and put them right.

should not be postponed. Planes and rasps which are used in the next stage are suitable for smoothing shapes already defined by the gouge, and are frustrating tools to use for first shaping. It is hard to decide whether to take a step 'backwards' to improve an aspect of the work once it has passed into the finishing and smoothing stages, but it is worth bearing in mind that once you have noticed a flaw that can be rectified, you will never be completely satisfied with what you have done until it is put right.

Smoothing the back

The small plane with the slightly convex blade is the most useful tool to use. Set this to a fine cut and guide it round the line of the purfling, shaving all gouge marks to the same level. Then, from the top of the arching work downwards, fanning out from each end, clean away the remaining ridges left by the gouges.

Hold the plane lightly and use it in the direction of the grain. In most cases this means that the planing direction should be from the top of the arching downwards. But at the ends and in the complex shaping of the arching at the inner bouts, the direction of the grain should be taken into account. Do not force the plane into the wood – if the blade digs in and tears out the grain, the time spent taking the whole surface back to hide the fault easily eliminates any gains made by working fast.

Feeling the back, in the manner shown, will help to reveal unevennesses. Gouges are by far the quickest and most effective way of establishing the shape. Remedial measures

Check continually for shape and symmetry. Remove all the ridges and do not stop smoothing the surface of the back until only very slight undulations can be felt. These are removed quickly and easily with the saw rasp described on page 20.

Rasping the surface

Take the saw rasp and, holding it firmly in both hands, bend the blade to suit the profile of the back. Rasp the back until even the slightest undulations have been removed and the back is reduced to a rough but regular shape. The saw rasp can be used with a direct push, but it can also be given a sideways diagonal thrust as well, which removes mounds and bumps more quickly than the direct thrust. However, when using this diagonally, make sure that the rasp does not dig in, leaving an embarrassing sawcut on the surface. Stop rasping when the back is levelled all over and the sides are a regular thickness.

Scrapers

The scrapers remove the toothmarks left by the rasp and prepare the back for sanding.

All of the marks left by the saw rasp must be removed at this stage. Work with the slope of the back and with the grain as much as possible. Remember always to start and finish the sweep of the scraper off the work, maintaining a smooth easy action through the sweep of each stroke. Once the worst of the marks have been

removed, and only slight depressions and scratches remain, finish with a razor blade sharpened to a hook.

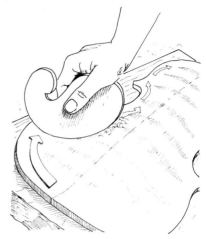

Sanding

Inspect the back very closely. There should be no scratches left by the saw rasp and only the slightest marks left by the scrapers. If any but the most superficial marks remain, remove them with scrapers before sanding.

Choose one sheet of 150 and one of 220 grit abrasive paper and a short length of stiff leather. Cut a couple of leather pads from the strap, each one measuring about 2 x 1 in and cut one or two strips of sandpaper, each sheet to fit round the leather pads.

Gripping the pads with the sandpaper, smooth the surface of the back, eliminating all the small scratches. Use the 150 grit first, working diagonally to the line of the grain. Finish with the 220 grit, with the grain. Dust the work periodically to check the finish. Once the back is sanded, take care of it; handle and store it carefully to prevent bruising and scratching.

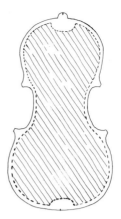

Hollowing the back

The plans show how the thicknesses of a violin back vary. The thickest part is the centre of the back, which extends on one side to the area of the soundpost. The thicknesses gradually diminish to a point just inside the ribs and end blocks. You must make every effort to avoid creating 'hard spots' in the structure of the instrument; thus, from the girder section at the sides there is a gradual reduction to the thinnest part just inside the purfling line. Linings are tapered into the sides and, at the point where the soundpost rests against the back, the slight extra thickness will be noted. The avoidance of hard spots in the back and in other parts of the instrument improves strength and flexibility, and, in consequence, the resonance of the sounding boards.

The task of carving the back to a thickness of $^3/_{16}$ in and less may seem daunting. But if work starts from the thickest point in the centre to the edges, you have ample time to perfect your skills before you gouge areas of critical thickness.

Marking out
The illustration shows what marks will be needed around the edge of the instrument. The shapes for the corner and end blocks are already marked on the plans obtainable from suppliers. For those who make their own, it is a simple matter. With a pencil, rough in on the template clean convex curves on the end blocks, and a gentle following curve on the corner blocks. Align the template with the back, and prick these curves through. Join these marks freehand. Run a pencil $^1/_4$ in in from the outside line of the instrument, to mark the limit of the carving at the perimeter.

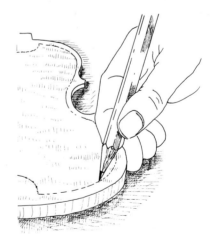

Carving
Carving the wood from the back of the violin is the most physically demanding and slowest of the operations required in making the

instrument, and it is worth ensuring that the working conditions are as favourable as possible. Note that the interior surface of the instrument is as smooth and as regular as the exterior. This is necessary for the resonance of the backboard. There should be no compromises in quality in the inaccessible areas. Even in the most secret parts of the instrument, the standard of workmanship and finish should be very high.

The back is placed on a bed of shavings in the carving box, with the flat inside face of the back flush with the top of the box. Some leather or timber tabs hold the edge of the fiddle from lifting out. If the maker prefers to stand while he works, the box should be fixed to the bench, with the work within easy reach of the edge. (I prefer to clamp the box to two trestles, which I straddle in order to lean into the carving.) Lighting must be excellent, gouges extremely sharp, with the strop and thickness gauge close by. Choose a good radio play or a ball game to listen to, and start carving.

The illustrations show the order for hollowing the back. The first step is to reduce the back to an even ¼ in thickness and then to carve the perimeter to the finished thickness. With the back resting its two side bouts against the wall of the carving box, gouge a line of cuts across the centreline. Once the full length of the back has been carved, start a second row a little further back and carve beneath the first cuts with each stroke. Continue gradually towards

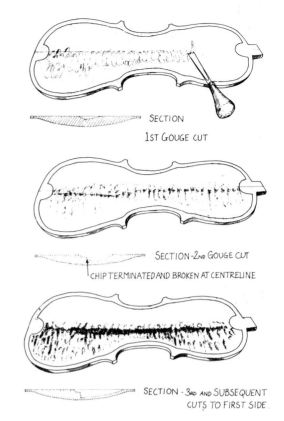

SECTION
1ST GOUGE CUT

SECTION - 2ND GOUGE CUT

CHIP TERMINATED AND BROKEN AT CENTRELINE

SECTION - 3RD AND SUBSEQUENT CUTS TO FIRST SIDE.

the edges. No cut should be a big effort, and each cut should separate its own chip or shaving. Remember to strop the gouges between cuts.

While making the first cuts, and with plenty of reassuring thickness left in the wood, use the

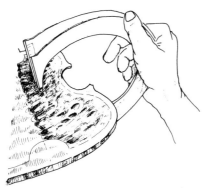

When the back is an even ¼ in thickness all over, begin to work at the thicknesses at the perimeter of the instrument. Work these down and carry the cuts right to the centre of the back, checking with the hand and gauge every few cuts. After working round the instrument once, change to a flatter gouge, and cut the ridges between the gouge marks. Carving should be methodical. Measure alternate cuts, resisting every temptation to make a cut unless you are certain of the wood's thickness.

gauge to check its thickness. Afterwards, feel the thickness with the thumb and fingers of the right hand. After a while you will discover a pleasure in feeling the delicacy of the shapes and in checking the hand measurement against that of the gauge. Although it is unwise to use your hands exclusively in the evaluation of thickness, during the roughing out of the inside back it can save a lot of time.

Once half of the back has been carved to approximately ¼ in thickness, turn the back round, and begin to reduce the other side. When carving, there is always a tendency for the tool to overshoot; control this by gripping the tip of the blade with your left hand (if right-handed). When starting on the second side, conditions are ideal for practising blade control, as there is an abrupt discrepancy between the levels in the centre of the back and each cut emerges in a direction which, if uncontrolled, can damage the side already carved. Bearing this in mind, work down the second side and across the top and bottom.

Having removed the ridges with the flat gouge, use the gauge to check for unevenness. The two most common areas neglected are between the inner bouts and just inside the end blocks. Now all areas must be reduced to their correct thickness. Mark in the high spots with a pencil – areas that are rather thin should be marked with red pencil. Circle in the soundpost position in red too, then pare away the high spots with the flat gouge.

The back should now feel light and thin, and within ¹⁄₁₆ in of its finished thickness all over. Take the most convex of the two small planes, and with the back still pressed into the shavings of the box, plane along the back and inwards down the arching from the sides. Follow with the flatter of the two planes and smooth the carved surface all over (except at the edges which must be left untouched). As the work nears completion, occasionally remove the back from the box, lay it on a flat surface, and gently press down on its back. At its correct thickness it should give slightly to gentle pressure.

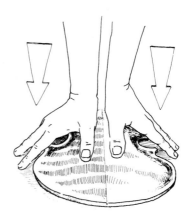

Check thicknesses and, with the planes or gouge, remove any major irregularities that remain. Then work over the face of the inside with the saw rasp. Check again with the gauge, and thin out any areas which remain too thick. Smooth the inside with suitable scrapers.

The belly

The sequence and techniques for shaping the belly are similar to those described on page 67. In describing an operation which has already been explained, page references are given for the relevant text or drawings.

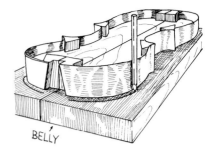

BELLY

Shaping the belly
When aligning the mould to the belly, remember to use the appropriate side of the mould. The slot for the neck, cut in the end block, widens out to the belly side of the mould and tapers towards the back. If the incorrect face of the mould is used for marking the outline of the belly, minor misalignments of the sides are doubled, and may cause difficulties when assembling the instrument. Remember that there will not be a button at the top of the belly.

Cutting
This is the same as for the back, but because of its greater tendency to split, take great care.

Preparation for carving
Attach the belly to the carving board.

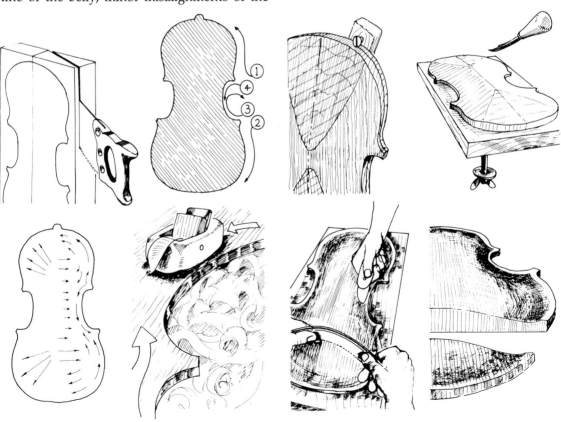

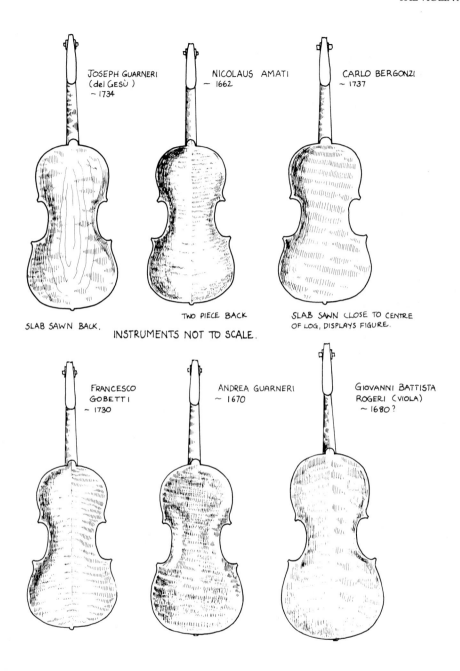

JOSEPH GUARNERI
(del GESÙ)
~ 1734

NICOLAUS AMATI
~ 1662

CARLO BERGONZI
~ 1737

SLAB SAWN BACK.

TWO PIECE BACK

SLAB SAWN CLOSE TO CENTRE
OF LOG, DISPLAYS FIGURE.

INSTRUMENTS NOT TO SCALE.

FRANCESCO
GOBETTI
~ 1730

ANDREA GUARNERI
~ 1670

GIOVANNI BATTISTA
ROGERI (VIOLA)
~ 1680?

Rough shaping
This is the same as for the back. Pine and spruce are more readily carved than the hardwood used for the back, and this stage will be completed quickly. However, the softwood is more likely to tear, splinter and split. Use very keen-edged tools in order to control these tendencies. Work slowly until you have the feel of the wood and are confident in your ability to predict the outcome of each stroke.

71

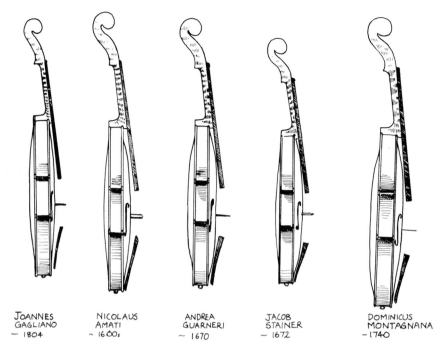

JOANNES
GAGLIANO
~ 1804

NICOLAUS
AMATI
~ 1600s

ANDREA
GUARNERI
~ 1670

JACOB
STAINER
~ 1672

DOMINICUS
MONTAGNANA
~ 1740

INSTRUMENTS NOT TO SCALE

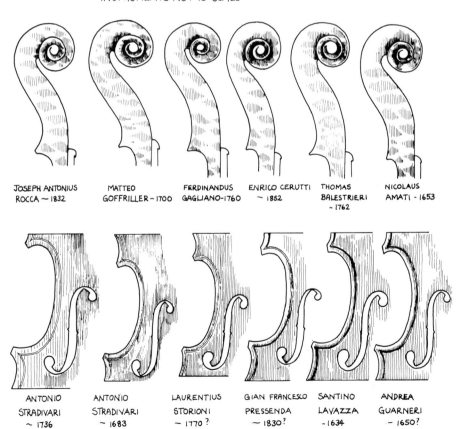

JOSEPH ANTONIUS
ROCCA ~ 1832

MATTEO
GOFFRILLER ~ 1700

FERDINANDUS
GAGLIANO ~ 1760

ENRICO CERUTTI
~ 1852

THOMAS
BALESTRIERI
~ 1762

NICOLAUS
AMATI ~ 1653

ANTONIO
STRADIVARI
~ 1736

ANTONIO
STRADIVARI
~ 1683

LAURENTIUS
STORIONI
~ 1770 ?

GIAN FRANCESCO
PRESSENDA
~ 1830?

SANTINO
LAVAZZA
~ 1634

ANDREA
GUARNERI
~ 1650?

Smoothing the belly

The rough shaping will have raised a slight lip to the edge of the sides of the belly, which is easily marred by the planes, rasps and scrapers used in the finishing of the shaping. Take great care, particularly at the edges, to ensure that the edges remain well defined and crisply shaped.

Scraping

Scrapers will not work well on softwoods unless they are extremely sharp.

Marking and drilling the f holes

The f holes can be marked and the holes which terminate each f hole can be bored at this stage. Alternatively, postpone the task of marking and cutting the f holes until the back is hollowed to its final thicknesses. The advantage of starting work on the holes at this stage is that the holes bored before the belly is hollowed are a help in determining the thicknesses when carving. If this operation is left until the belly is thinned, the entire f hole shape will have to be partially cut with a fretsaw, which can be a rather awkward business.

There are several advantages in leaving the cutting until the thicknessing is complete. One is that the f holes are such an important feature that to define them so early in the construction of the belly may curtail the maker's opportunity to formulate the most satisfactory shape for them. Of more relevance to the beginner are the advantages that the marks need only be drawn once if the cutting is accomplished later, and that the edges to the holes already bored may be damaged in the carving of the inside of the belly. Especially to begin with, it is probably best to bore the holes at this stage.

If you look closely at the variety of f hole shapes depicted in this book and try to copy them freehand, you will realize that they are an extremely subtle shape, and depressingly difficult to draw. As with the profile, scroll and pegbox, the best way to study the shape is to copy a good one. Notice the variations in design and size and position of the f holes illustrated here: they bracket the bridge and extend longitudinally and across the instrument, allowing a certain independence of movement between

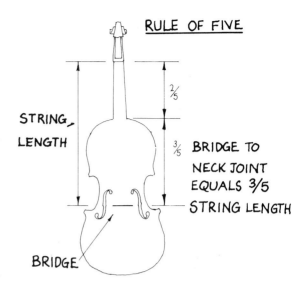

the upper and the lower bouts of the belly. Incisions in the belly to make the f holes are all curved; those with the round terminations of the established design are shaped to resist cracking and to prevent the introduction of stress points in the belly.

The drawing below is a template of a full-sized violin f hole with the sides and the violin centreline marked in. The nicks in the side represent the locating marks for the bridge. The nick in the centreline gives an additional reference mark when marking the second f hole on the opposite side of the instrument.

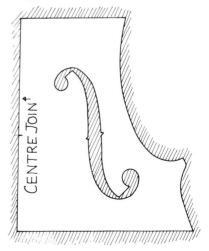

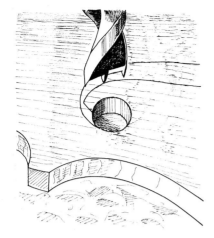

Take a brad-point drill a little smaller than the diameter of the lower lobes of the f holes, and fit it in the chuck of an electric drill. With the drill held perpendicular to the surface, drill into the belly. Repeat for the other side, then with a smaller diameter drill for the two upper lobes. You do not need to do anything else to the f holes at this stage, but they can be used as a useful reference for gauging the thickness of the belly when hollowing it out.

Establish the correct location of the template, and with a sharp pencil draw around the f hole shape, and also mark the centreline nick on the belly. Change the template to the other side, and mark it there too.

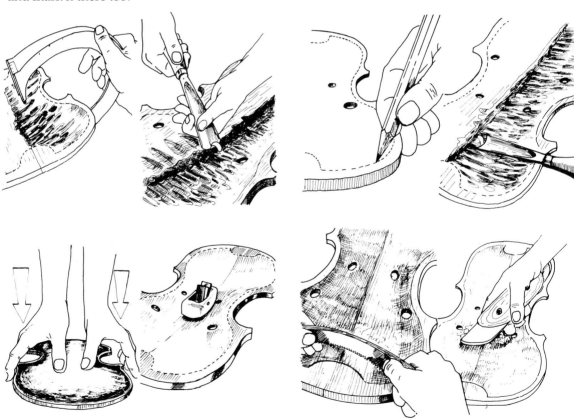

Hollowing the belly

Only hollow the belly whilst it is supported by the carving box. Handle the belly delicately. Its edges and corners, in particular, are very vulnerable. Use extremely sharp tools and be wary of the temptation to cut along the grain. It is quicker, but more difficult, to cut cleanly and to avoid splitting ahead of the gouge. Refer to the plans for guidance when carving the belly. Note the slight reinforcement at the soundpost. Experiment to discover the optimum thickness by testing its spring, described in detail below.

Place the belly face down on a flat surface and apply moderate pressure to the centreline. The belly should flex slightly. Place your thumbs on the upper bouts and press as illustrated. The belly should resist the pressure, but give slightly. Repeat for the lower bouts. If the belly is too stiff, check the thicknesses are all correct, and remove more wood around the perimeter with a flat gouge, saw rasp or scrapers. If only the finest reduction in thickness is looked for, rub 90 grit paper over the inside face. This rough paper will score the surface, which can then be scraped and sanded clean – a fine, even thickness having been removed.

Smoothing and finishing

Use very sharp scrapers. Remember that the pine is very easily scored. Although bumps on the inside may be invisible they may nevertheless detract from the resonance of the finished instrument.

Hold the finished belly between thumb and first finger at its balancing point. Tap the belly gently with a finger of the left hand, and listen to the resonance. The note should be clean and clear. If it is not, check over the belly for cracks, splits and a poor glue join in the centre.

Problems and remedies

Poor glue join

Unless the join is very bad it is preferable not to have to reglue it. It is usually sufficient to run hot glue into slight crevices inside the fiddle and fit small studs across the joint. Heat the glue and thin it slightly. When the water in the glue pot is hot and the glue is ready to use, brush a little hot water onto the crack and follow this with hot glue. Use the thin glue knife to work the glue into the join; leave it to chill before cleaning the inside with hot water.

Cutting and fitting the studs

Small studs which bridge the joint in the back and belly add to the strength considerably, without detracting from the resonance of the instrument. Select a small piece of close and straight-grained quarter-sawn pine, and cut it to a width of ¼ in. Square off the end, and then mark round a cutting line ¼ in in from the end.

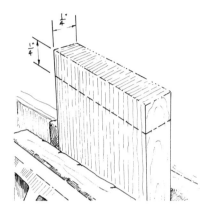

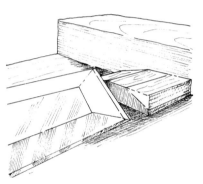

Resting each stud against the bench hook, chisel them to the finished shape as illustrated above. Chisel along the grain first, before finishing the bevelling with the two side cuts at

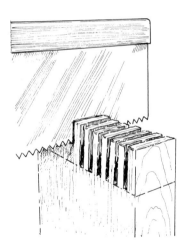

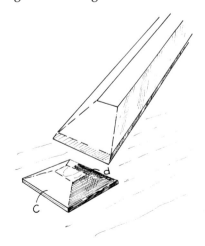

Place the piece, end up, in the vice and saw downwards to the line with a backsaw. The sawcut should be between the hard summer growth lines in the grain. Saw as many as possible, each saw cut about 1/16 in apart. After 12 or so cuts, place the piece across a bench hook and saw off the small slips of timber in one go.

c and *d*. After each stud has been cut and shaped, sand it lightly to remove roughness and store the studs until they are required.

Studs are fitted across butt joins, their grain direction perpendicular to the grain of the pieces being joined. Because they are so small, the best way to handle them is to prick them with a pointed tool such as a knife or a compass.

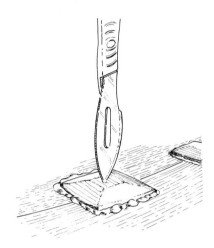

Apply slightly thinned glue to the flat surface while they remain impaled on the point and press them gently across the joint. Hold them for a few moments until the glue has chilled and then twist and lift away the tool. Brush away excess glue with warm water and a stiff brush. Space the studs no closer than one inch apart.

Cracks

If a crack is discovered in the belly or any other part of the main body of the instrument, it will have to be glued and then studded, as described above. With most cracks it is possible to run glue over the crack and then, by manipulating the crack, work the glue into it. Fit studs across the crack.

Reinforcing the belly

Sometimes an area is carved or planed too thin and needs to be rebuilt. If the area is small, and the shaving which was taken from it is still available, then all that needs to be done is to glue the shaving back into place in the manner described below. For larger areas, the surface will have to be smoothed to a regular finish before fitting the patch.

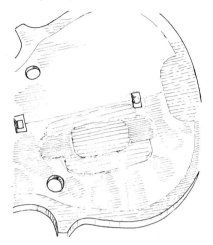

Find or cut some thin pine shavings (for the belly) or hardwood shavings for the back, and press them into position. Several layers may be required to restore the belly to its correct thickness; fit and glue these separately. Cut the shaving roughly to size, and press it into place to check its fit. If, owing to the double curve of the area to be rebuilt, the patch refuses to lie closely to the belly, score its underside with a razor to weaken it. Once the patch fits over the

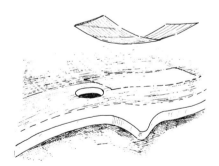

thin spot, place the belly back in the carving box and snuggle it into the box, until it is evenly supported by the shavings. Take a pad of closed cell polyethylene foam, Plasticine (modelling clay) or felt, and press it against the patch. Arrange a bar and weights, or elastic, across the carving box to give sufficient pressure to ensure a uniform bond.

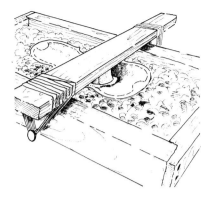

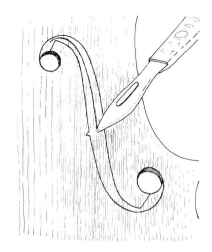

Apply glue to the belly and the patch and then press the patch into place. Cover it with a sheet of clear plastic or covering film. Place the pressure pad into position and press it with the bar fixed across the carving box. Leave it for the glue to harden. If a larger area than one inch has to be patched, the reinforcement pieces will have to be laid in strips about ¾ in wide, each strip laid in a separate operation. Do not level the repair until the glue has hardened.

Carving the f holes
Once the belly is finished on the inside, take the f hole template, fit it over the holes drilled in the belly and remark the line for the f holes.

Take a sharp scalpel and, with the belly lying flat on the bench, make a cut from the top lobe to the bottom, running the cut roughly down the centre of the f hole. Do not press hard. Use these initial, cautious cuts to gain a feel for the wood. Make a second cut close to the first, and if both are cut at the angle illustrated, a small splinter of wood will be released. Continue to widen and deepen the groove until the knife cuts right through the belly.

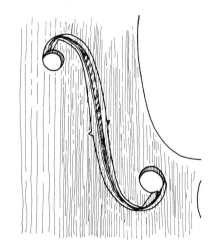

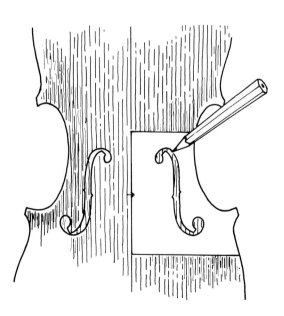

As soon as the incision connects the lobes, take up the belly and rest it against your chest, with its face side uppermost. Slip the knife underneath, and with the blade pointing towards you, begin to shave away one side of the incision.

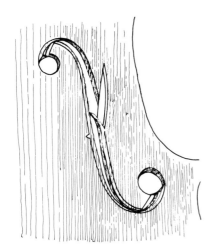

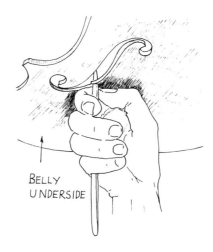

If you look closely at the f hole marked on the belly, you will note that the grain direction and attitude of the f holes make it possible to trim one side of the f hole in one direction; if, however, the knife is used in the wrong direction, it is difficult to control and the belly will split. The illustration of the f hole with the cutting direction marked on it demonstrates this.

Trim one side of the f hole, reverse the belly and cut down the second side. If necessary, clean the line with a small slither of wood, wrapped with sandpaper. Use a round file at the ends.

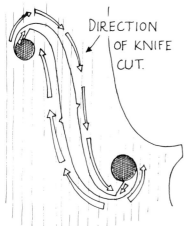

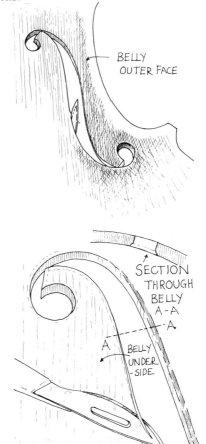

Hold the knife as illustrated. For vertical control use the thumb as a fence by resting it against the underside of the belly. Braking is achieved by raising the side of the first finger against the belly. If the flat of the blade bears against the part of the f hole that has just been cut, shavings rather than splinters will be removed.

Because the f holes on each side of the fiddle cross the thickness contours of the belly, a variation in thickness will be visible at the edges of the hole. Take the knife again, and having located the thinnest part of the edge work along the inside edge of the f hole, make a slight chamfer so that the apparent belly width is standard throughout the length of the f hole.

Fretsawing the f holes

Mark the f holes as described on page 78. Support the interior of the belly against a cork block or pad and use a bradawl or drill to puncture the belly in the centre of each lobe.

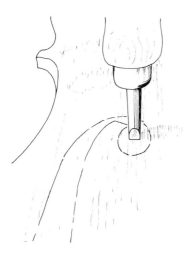

Ensure that the chisel end of the bradawl cuts across the line of the grain, otherwise the belly will split. Clamp the scroll sawing board in the

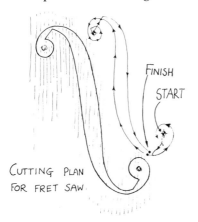

vice, overhanging the side of the bench, and slip the fine blade of the scroll saw through one of the bradawl holes in the belly. Tension the blade in the upper arm clamp of the scroll saw.

With very small vertical cuts, saw around the inside of the marks for the circular lobe. Then saw down the middle of the f hole to the lobe at the other end of the hole. Saw the circle at this end and withdraw the blade. Saw the second f hole in a similar way and trim it with a knife. Because of the difficulties of sawing cleanly through grain that is alternately hard and then soft, it will be necessary to work a circular file into each lobe before finishing the carving.

The bass bar

Before the instrument is assembled, the bass bar must be glued to the inside of the belly. The illustration above shows the size and position

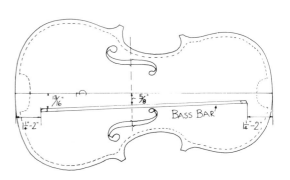

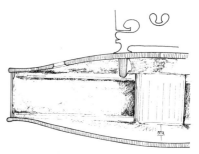

of the bar relative to the belly. The section shows that the bass bar lies directly beneath the left (bass) foot of the bridge. This is the only strut fitted inside the instrument. It should be made from close and straight-grained pine, and fitted perfectly to the inside curves of the belly.

two lumps at each end and force them gently against the bar to hold it while it is marked for fitting. Take a small strip of strap leather and, with the pencil resting upon it, draw down each side of the bar.

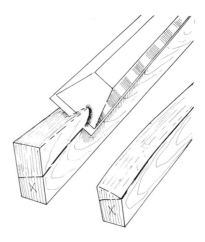

The dimensions given here are included to serve as a guide. Because of the natural discrepancies in strengths and stiffness between different samples of pine, the size of the bar will vary from instrument to instrument (just as the thicknesses will vary from fiddle to fiddle, according to the maker's assessment of the wood). In general, the stronger the bar, the harder and the tighter will be the tone and response.

Choose a piece of suitable pine and position it so that the annual rings are perpendicular to the face of the belly. Once its orientation is established, cut it to size, leaving a little additional wood for the depth of the bass bar in case more wood is taken off in fitting than was anticipated. Mark on the inside of the belly the exact position for the bar. Note that the bass bar and centreline of the belly converge slightly. To avoid confusion, make an identifying mark on the end grain of the top of the bass bar and define its angle and longitudinal position on the belly.

Place the bar in the vice. Refer to one set of side marks only and cut a bevel to the line. Then refer to the second set of marks and the edge of the bevel, and shave down to the line.

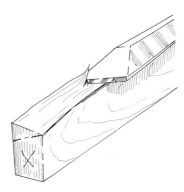

Fitting the bass bar
Take some small lumps of warm Plasticine (modelling clay). Set the bass bar over its marks and hold it in its correct vertical attitude. Place

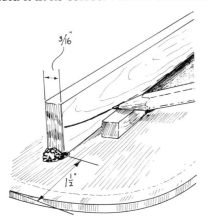

Fit the bass bar again, this time without the Plasticine, and inspect the joint. It will need more work.

Take some chalk and rub it along the line of the bass bar in the belly. Replace the bar and rub it longitudinally for about 1/16 in in each direction. Lift away the bar and shave off the chalk marks. Repeat and shave away the marks again. With care, the area of close contact will increase and the chalk mark will spread further

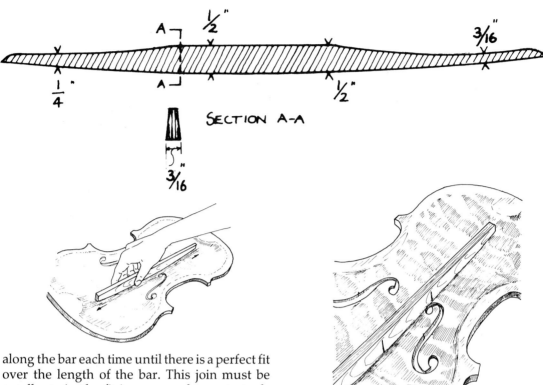

SECTION A-A

along the bar each time until there is a perfect fit over the length of the bar. This join must be excellent. As the fit improves, change to tools which take a finer cut. Use a chisel to begin with, then change to a plane and set the iron to an increasingly fine cut as the fitting progresses. Provided that when it is fitted the attitude and position of the bar remain constant, each cut will improve the fit.

Pre-stress the belly by springing the bar into place. This requires a little additional shaping, taking a little more wood from just beyond its area of maximum strength (which is that part between the f holes) to the ends.

Mark with a pencil the area of the bass bar which lies beneath the f hole and then replace the bar in the vice with its glueing face uppermost. Set a small plane to its finest cut and, starting from one of the marks near the centre of the bar, make a delicate cut to the end. Repeat at the other end. Starting again from the first mark, measure off approximately 1¼ in and starting there, shave to the end. Continue working outwards, remembering always to maintain the angles so painstakingly acquired earlier. Repeat at the other end.

Remove the bar and place it in position. With a little pressure it may be possible to press the belly against the bar, but before glueing the bass bar has to be cut and shaped so that it, too, will spring into the necessary curve.

Using the illustration as a guide, mark on the

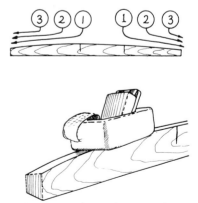

82

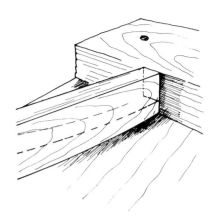

Assembly

With the exception of trimming and purfling the edges, the work on the back and belly is virtually complete, and as soon as the sides and blocks are prepared the instrument can be assembled.

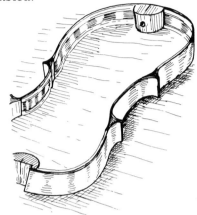

bar its finished shape and, with the bench hook to steady the bar, cut it to shape with a chisel. Bevel the sides with the plane and finish by rounding off the corners with sandpaper. Taper the ends so that they appear to melt into the belly.

Glueing the bass bar

Make two bass bar clamps as illustrated, and keep a couple of spring hand clamps or some thick rubber bands close by. Heat the glue, size both the bar and the position of the bar, and wipe off. Apply hot glue to the bass bar, and press it into place. Slip the clamp over the belly so that one block rests against the end of the bass bar and the other side bears against the top of the belly. Slip a hand clamp across the two arms, or twist some rubber bands over the ends.

Trimming the end and corner blocks

These blocks must be trimmed from the dovetail sections which hold them in the mould into smooth curves which reflect the curves of the interior of the violin. These curves are marked on the template for the back and belly and were used in defining the edge limits for hollowing the back and belly.

Place the mould on the workbench. Adjust the template over the mould until the sides and centrelines are aligned. At the ends and corners of the template are marks for defining the

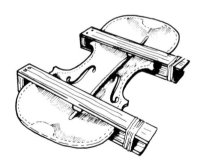

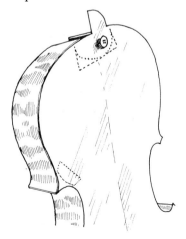

Repeat at the other end. Use the hot wet glue brush to wipe away surplus glue and leave to dry. When the glue is thoroughly hardened, work over all the surfaces with some fine 220 paper to remove roughness.

blocks. Prick through these marks to transfer them to the end grain of the corner and end blocks. Turn the mould over and repeat for the other side.

Once the blocks have been marked, tap out the mould from the sides with a light hammer. Take a sharp chisel and, with the side assembly on a cutting board and with reference to the marks drawn on the end block, pare down the end block almost to the lines marked in from the template. Turn the mould over and trim it to the precise line marked on the end grain. Shape the second end block and then the corner blocks. The inside face of the corner blocks should follow the curves of the inner and outer bouts and so will have to be cut out with a flat chisel, followed with a flat gouge.

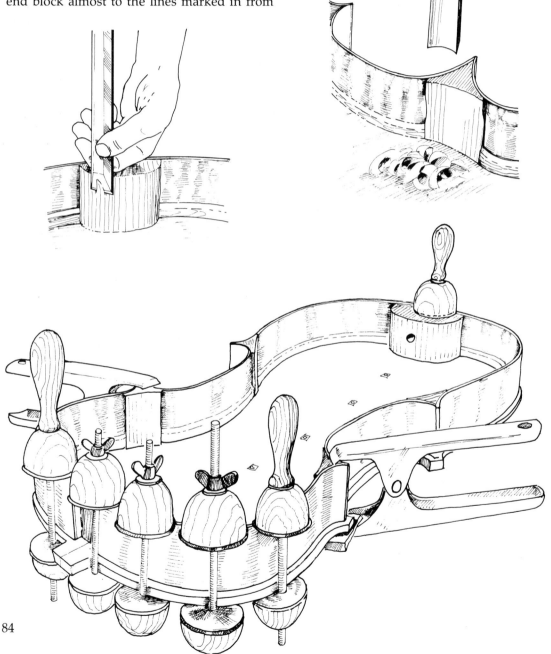

Glueing the back to the sides

Once the sides have been released from the mould, it is a good idea to glue them to the back as soon as possible. Check the back and the end blocks and redraw the centrelines if they have been obliterated or smudged by the previous work.

Take the screw clamps described on page 24 and position the sides over the back. Since the sides will have sprung out of their tight curves once the constraints of the mould have been removed, each part will have to be pulled gently into position and held with a screw clamp. You need a large number of clamps to glue the back in one operation – six for the inner bouts and 16 for the outer bouts, as well as additional clamps at the top and bottom end blocks.

It simplifies matters to have sufficient clamps, but they are quite expensive and it is possible to achieve an equally satisfactory result by using a combination of about six violin screw clamps and a couple of spring grips and by only glueing a small portion of the sides at a time. The procedure is the same for both situations, but the latter will take a little longer and is described below.

Heat the glue and place the thin glue knife in the water to warm. Apply thinned glue as a size to the end grain of the blocks and to the linings. Position the end blocks as accurately as possible, making sure that the centrelines match and that the blocks are the correct distance in from the ends. Once the end blocks

are in position, use the remaining screws and clamps to hold down the rest of the sides. If only a few clamps remain, put a clamp each side of the top block and then concentrate the remainder on one upper bout, reserving one clamp to hold the top block and another to pull the inner bout into place.

Check alignments to make sure that the top block is central and that, as far as it is possible to determine, it is not biased to one side or the other. Then prepare to glue. Remove the clamp holding the top block and loosen the adjacent clamp, and take the glue knife and dip it into the gluepot. Slip the knife between the back and the end block and apply glue to both faces. Replace the end block clamp and tighten it. If enough glue has been used, a little surplus glue should show at the edges of the join. Remove the adjacent clamp and loosen the next, and repeat the procedure, working round towards the corner that has been clamped. Do not glue the corner, unless there are enough clamps to continue into the inner bout. If there are not enough then leave the glue to set and return to it when the clamps can be removed without any likelihood that the glue join will come apart. Wash away surplus glue with the stiff-haired glue brush dipped in hot water.

Work towards the centre bouts and then from the bottom block upwards, finishing with the centre bout. Repeat on the other side, making sure to leave a sufficient margin at the edges to allow trimming. When the sides and blocks are fixed, clean away excess glue with a razor blade and finish with sandpaper.

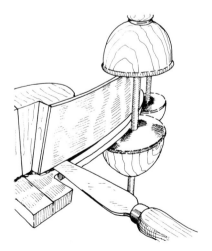

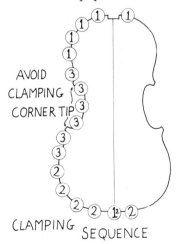

AVOID CLAMPING CORNER TIP

CLAMPING SEQUENCE

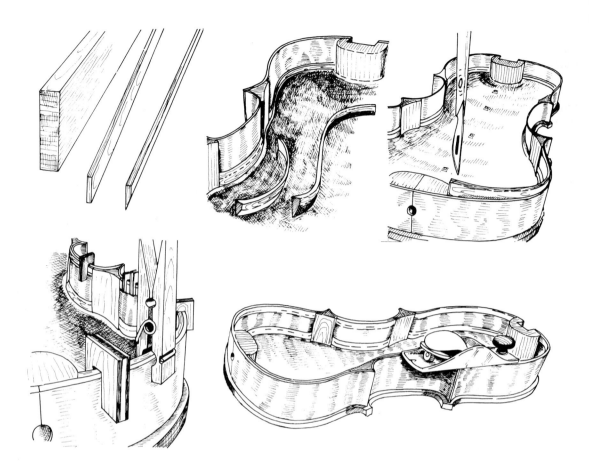

Fitting the linings

Once the back is glued, the belly should be fitted as soon as possible, before changes in temperature, humidity or the stresses locked into the structure cause the back to warp. The linings for the belly are fitted in precisely the same way as the linings which are fitted against the back (see page 57). Once the linings are fitted to the sides of the instrument, plane them flush with the corner blocks and the sides.

Fitting the belly

When the violin needs adjustments or repairs, it is usually the belly which is removed in order to gain access to the interior of the instrument. Because of this, it is traditional for a thinner glue to be used to fasten the belly than the back, and it is also, for this reason, a good idea to slip

a strip of newspaper between the sides and the belly.

Take a sheet of newspaper and lay it on a flat board. Apply thinned glue to the glueing edge of the instrument and press the sides against the paper. Invert and press the paper down onto the edge of the sides. When the glue has dried, use a sharp knife to cut round the outline

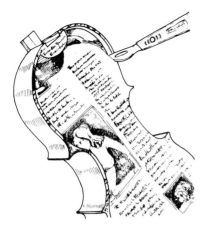

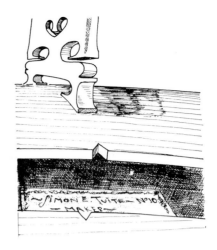

of the belly to remove surplus paper and also to cut away any paper inside the linings and blocks.

With the paper glued and trimmed so that only the very finest strip remains glued to the sides, and with the interior of the instrument clean and sanded smooth all round, prepare to fit the belly.

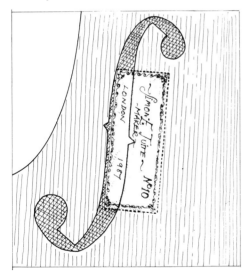

Before doing so, make up a maker's label and fit it to the back of the violin, in a position which is easily visible when viewed through the left side f hole. Sign, date and number the instruments if they represent experiments for which you are keeping specifications. Heat the glue and, when it is liquid, dilute it so that it is twice as thin as usual. Fit the belly in exactly the same

way as the back, but remember that there will be no opportunity to clean the interior of the instrument once it is assembled. Use only the minimum of glue and apply it with great care to avoid it running down the sides. Wash away surplus glue from the outside and sandpaper the edges and sides when the glue has dried.

Trimming the edge

The violin is now nearly complete. All that remains is to trim and purfle the edges of the instrument before shaping and fitting the neck.

Sit with the violin resting in your lap with a sharp penknife, small plane and the outline template for reference close by. Plane and

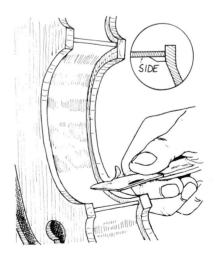

SIDE

whittle the sawn edges of the back and belly to a regular and graceful shape ⅛ in beyond the curved sides. It is very important that the curves, particularly at the corners, are graceful, and a slight departure from the sides is acceptable here.

Try to ensure that the shape of the belly is echoed by the shape of the back. In carving the one, check the other side to see that there is enough wood in both edges before carving the first. When carving the second side refer constantly to the first to ensure that the copy is accurate.

Once the outlines of the back and belly have been trimmed, level the convex curves with a file and the hollows with a stiff leather pad wrapped with sandpaper. Leave the button irregular until after the neck is fitted and shaped. Take the penknife and cut a bevel round the inside edges adjacent to the sides as illustrated. Cut a small outer bevel and round it with a file and sandpaper. Finish the edge with 220 grit paper held against a slip of leather strap with a groove gouged in it.

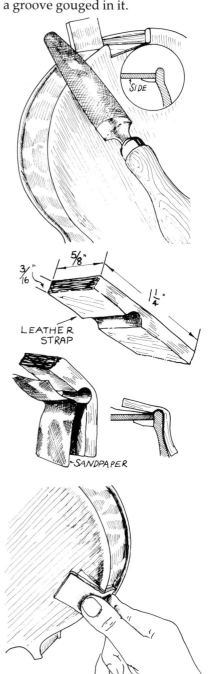

Purfling

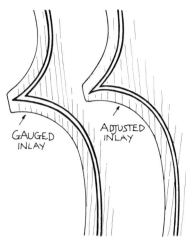

Purfling is the very narrow inlay banding, usually consisting of a thin white core, sandwiched between two thinner strips of pearwood, stained black. Purfling can be made in the home workshop and it can also be bought

Since the inlay is marked in freehand at the button anyway, it is recommended that the corners are given the same freehand embellishment.

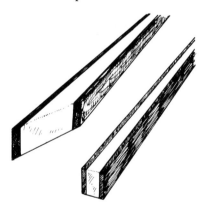

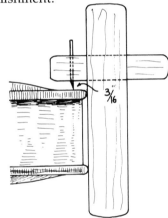

from the suppliers listed at the back. Instructions for making your own purfling are included later on page 137. In this section, it is assumed that the purfling is purchased from the supplier ready made.

Although it is not a necessary refinement, purfling will decorate and strengthen the edges of the instrument. The purfling is gauged parallel to the edges, but the corners look more attrative if it deviates slightly, as illustrated above. Any deviation from the edge of the fiddle has to be cut freehand to clear marks.

Before marking the inlay line on the violin, practise on an offcut of planed hardwood. Set the purfling cutter with the bevel of the cutter facing away 3/16 in from its fence. Make certain that the wedges are all in tight and then practise running the cutter against the edge of the practice piece.

The cutter is held as illustrated overleaf, with the fence resting against the two edges of the instrument. Draw it down the face of the offcut. Without pressing hard, make a well-defined incision into which the point of the scalpel can slip. Try the cutter across the more disruptive end grain of the offcut to gain a feel for the cutter as it bumps across the hard late growth.

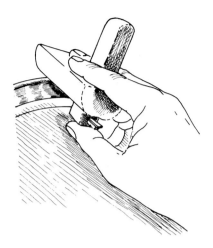

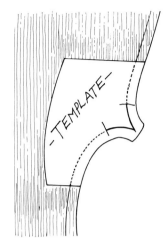

Mark at the corners the areas where the purfling diverges from the edges. The pencil line is to mark the limit for the cutter. Take the cutter and start on the back. With firm pressure against the fence and a little vertical pressure run the cutter round the edges. It will spoil the line to go over it a second time unless the line deviates accidentally from the edge. When the back edges have been marked, repeat for the belly. This may be rather more difficult, as the variable density of the wood makes control of the cutter less predictable.

Pencil these onto the card and use the cutter to mark in the purfling to this point. Then, with a pencil, drawing freehand or with the help of some random curves cut from card, draw in the sweep of the purfling to the corner as illustrated. Cut this line with the scalpel and use it as a template for pencilling in the corners.

The short length of purfling in the shadow of the button can usually be marked using a similar tracing of the curve of the bottom of the instrument.

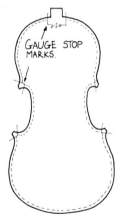

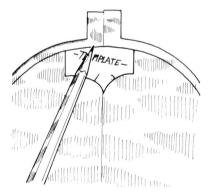

Marking in the corners and the button
Take a filing card and press it against one of the corners of the violin. Trace round the edge of the violin at a corner. Cut along the line to make a template. Above and below each corner will be marks drawn to limit the purfling cutter.

Once there is a continuous pencil and gauged line round the front and back of the violin, take a scalpel and incise the line, resting the scalpel in the cut made by the purfling cutter. At the button and the corners, the scalpel is used freehand. Keep the cut vertical, and work down the knife cut until it is about 1/16 in deep. It is easiest to cut small radius corners with the hand on the inside of the curve, pivoting the blade against a

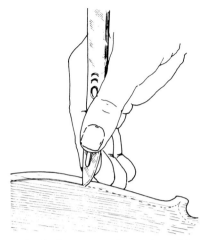

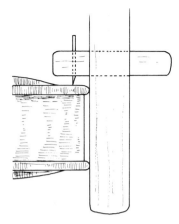

finger which bears against the side of the instrument.

Although the wood is harder, the back is easier to mark than the belly, where uneven densities make knife control difficult. Incising the purfling is probably one of the most worrying operations in making the fiddle.

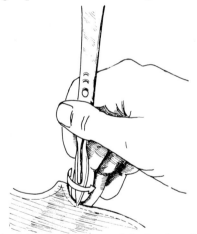

Remember that the surface of the back and belly at the purfling is still to be sunk, so that the slight bruising and slips of the knife, although disheartening, will probably not show up when the instrument is finished. Never extemporize with the line. Press firmly but not so hard that the knife sticks. Do not try to rescue a deviation from the line by carrying on. Faults in cutting the purfling lines are not usually difficult to conceal (some methods are mentioned at the conclusion of this section).

Once the first cut is made all around the front and back of the violin, readjust the cutter so that its sharpening bevel is facing the fence, and set it to the additional width of the purfling strip. Tighten up the wedges and test the cutter on the original practice offcut. Hold a strip of purfling over the two grooves made by the cutter and, if necessary, readjust the postion of the fence until the purfling fits the lines. Take the scalpel and deepen both cuts. Remove the waste with the very fine purfling chisel described on page 121, slip the sample length of purfling into the groove and make the necessary adjustments to the fence if the fit is unsatisfactory.

Once the cutter has been set, repeat the marking procedure around the edges of the instrument. Use the same template for marking in the corners and button and cut around again with the scalpel, making sure that the deepening cuts remain vertical. Take particular

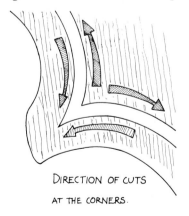

DIRECTION OF CUTS

AT THE CORNERS.

91

care at the corners where the cuts should be made in the direction illustrated with the hand in the centre of the arc.

Once the line is cut, work between the cuts in the back with the purfling chisel, lifting out the waste and levelling the floor of the groove. Leave the very tip of the corners until the rest of the groove has been cleaned and levelled, and then remove the small residue of waste with the scalpel.

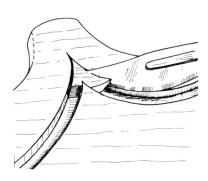

Fitting the purfling

This is a straightforward operation provided that the groove is the correct width. Take a short length of purfling and test it in the groove. It should slide into the groove without difficulty. If the fit is too tight, trim the purfling to the correct thickness, using the homemade trimmer illustrated on page 21, rather than try to widen the groove. If the groove is too wide, press ahead and fit the purfling. Even though at this stage it may look rather shoddy, it always

looks better once it is glued and pressed into place, with the tops sunk to their finished depth.

Fit the purfling around the top bouts of the belly. Unless the inlay is very narrow it will have to be bent to fit into the curve at the corners. This is easily done by dipping the tip of the purfling in hot glue water, then quickly pressing it against the side of the glue pot or hot bending iron until it is the correct shape.

With this fitting, it is better to slightly over-bend the purfling so that it presses hard against the outer side of the groove at the corners. Fit the strip and ease it into the groove. Mark it with a knife just short of the centreline in the middle (immediately over the slot for the neck), remove it, cut it off, then press it into position again. Repeat for the second upper bout and the two lower bouts.

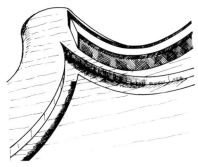

Fitting the purfling to the inner bouts is more difficult. Each requires two bends, and this doubles the chance of breaking the strip. Also, both ends have to be fitted, which means that they must be trimmed with the greatest of care. Bend the first end and trim its tip as illustrated.

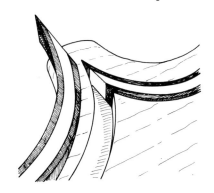

Continue bending the strip, if necessary brushing hot water onto it to soften it. Bend the second end as accurately as possible, easing it into shape until it sits precisely over the groove. Press the first end into position and work the inlay along the groove, until it rests directly over the second corner. Check that the fit is right all the way around the curve, particularly at the first end. Mark with the scalpel the exact position for the second cut. Remove the purfling and make the second cut, just a fraction further out than the scalpel mark.

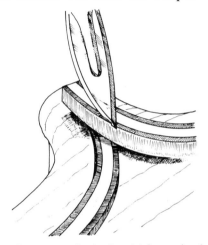

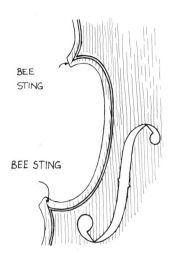

Replace the strip, which should fit perfectly. If it is too long, remove it and shave it away at its fine edge until it slides into the corner. At this stage the 'bee sting' can be cut in. Take the scalpel, and incise a line firmly in each corner, towards the edge of the instrument. Rub the tip of a soft (2B) pencil into the cut and then repeat at the other corners.

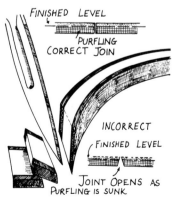

The back is inlaid in exactly the same way except that invisible joins have to be made in the purfling at the top and bottom. However, having made the mitred joins at the corners on the first side, the square joins close to the centreline of the back are straightforward, provided that they are cut square in all planes. Never bevel the purfling. As the top of the purfling is sunk, the joint will get worse. Fit the bouts in the same order. Butt the purfling as closely as possible, just short of the centreline on both the top and bottom of the back.

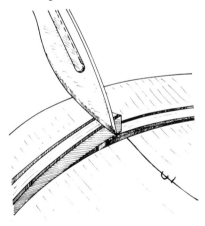

Glueing the purfling

Once all of the strips are fitted, lift out one side of the belly's purfling and, in reverse order to that in which they were fitted, run hot thinned glue into the groove of the inner bout and slip the purfling in place. Press the corners in first and then press the rest of the strip into the groove, adding glue if necessary. If the glue chills as the purfling is pressed in, heat a smooth piece of metal, such as a hammer head, and press the inlay with that. This liquefies the glue, and allows the purfling to sink to its correct depth. Lightly tap the inlay with the ball peen of a small metalwork hammer in those areas where the purfling is a loose fit, to widen the purfling to fill the groove. In quick succession, fit the top and bottom purfling.

On the longer strips, and where time is needed for fitting, apply glue only to the first part of the groove, and run more glue in with a knife or brush ahead of the strip as it is being laid. Continue this right round the instrument. If the purfling is very loose, mix some black pigment into the glue. When it dries, it will seem that the ebonized strip is slightly thicker at this point and will pass unnoticed when the work is cleaned up. If the fault is very bad, it is safer to mix fine sawdust into the glue and force it into the cavity after the purfling is in place.

Trimming

Once the glue has hardened, take a very sharp flat gouge, and with a swing arm lamp giving a strong low light, trim away all the glue residue and any inlay proud of the surface. Then strop the gouge, and work round the edge, first on the back and then the front, shaving away a thin slither of wood over the purfling. Once about 1/16 in has been removed all around on both sides, melt in the sides of the shallow

hollow by working at its edges, cleaning away any new bumps caused by the sinking. Because there is very little wood beneath the chisel, this must be carried out with the greatest of care, each cut planned before execution and each cut releasing it own fine shaving. Follow round with the small convex plane or saw file, and then finish with scrapers and sandpaper. Whichever tools are used, make certain that the tools do not damage the raised edges at the sides. Finish by dampening the front and back of the instrument. When it is dry, lightly sand over its face. It ought to be quite beautiful.

Trimming the purfling

Purfling which is of uneven thickness is extremely difficult to use. Alterations in thickness should be accomplished as accurately as possible. The illustration shows a device which is adjustable, and which will, if sharpened and handled carefully, reduce the

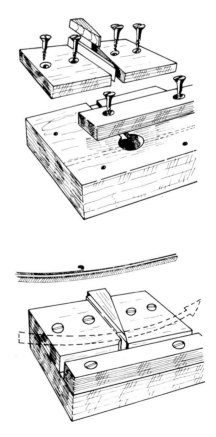

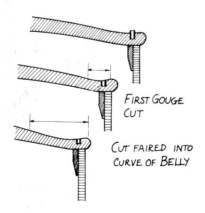

FIRST GOUGE CUT

CUT FAIRED INTO CURVE OF BELLY

inlay to a satisfactory and regular thickness. Remove only the smallest shavings at a time, otherwise the cutter will dig in and break the inlay.

The neck, pegbox and scroll

Carving the scroll

This is perhaps the only part of the process of violin making where the inexperienced maker may lose confidence and enthusiasm. Scroll carving can easily fall out of sequence and control. There are two reasons for this: one is that there are only minimal marks to help guide the chisel, and the other is that the scroll itself can be very confusing to carve.

If you have not recently carved or played with modelling clay, I would recommend that shortly before working on the scroll, you spend some idle hours working half scrolls in Plasticine until you are familiar with the shape. Model lots of one-sided scrolls rather than try to create a perfect example.

Because there are so few marks to guide the craftsman, it is very important that you stick rigidly to the ones you have, and if a mark is accidently cut away you restore or repair the piece before continuing. It is almost invariably the case that once one begins to deviate from the planned shape, the resulting scroll takes longer to finish and is less satisfactory than if one had stopped and repaired the mistake.

The plans will include a full-size profile of the neck and scroll, which can be cut out and used as a template. Also on page 41 there is a description of how to copy the outline of a scroll and neck from an existing model.

The drawings below show clearly the proportions and relation between the neck, scroll and body of the instrument. Select quarter-sawn sycamore for the neck with great care. All its surfaces must be clean and free of evidence of knots, varying grain density, cracks and other weaknesses. It should reveal a powerful figure when planed up.

The size required for a violin neck, pegbox and scroll is 11 x 1½ x 2in. There is an advantage in keeping some additional length to the neck to help in holding the scroll while it is being shaped.

Plane the block square, mark the face and edge sides. Test the face side for twist with a pair of winding sticks, and correct any bias before marking in the centreline on the face side, across the ends, and down the back. This line can be marked with a marking gauge.

Take the profile template, place it against the side of the block and pin it in place. Draw

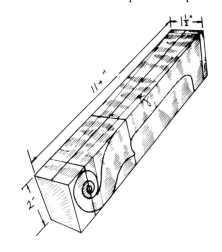

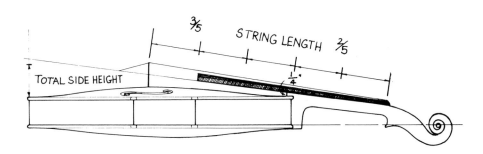

95

around the template with a pointed pencil and mark in the reference points for the top nut, scroll centre and the end of the neck.

With the template still in place, prick through the lines defining the curls of the scroll. Remove the template, and carefully join the prick marks freehand. This records the curl of the scroll on the first side. Square off reference points across the front face and down the opposite side. Mark down to the centre of the scroll on the first side, and mark this on the second side. Fit the template, align it to the marks on the second side and check it carefully before pinning it in position, drawing round it, and pricking the scroll.

When the sides are marked in, measure off from the plans the width and taper of the neck and transfer these dimensions to the front and back of the block. In some instruments this taper continues to the base of the scroll, but in others, including the example given in the plans, there is a slight swelling at the pegbox. Mark this and then draw in a line both at the front and back of the neck to signify the limit of the cut for the sides. If you have access to a bandsaw, then this is the ideal tool to use, otherwise use a handsaw, coping or bow saw to cut out the neck and scroll. Cut in the sequence described below.

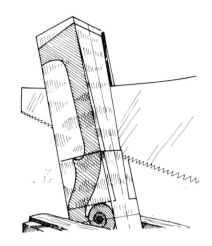

SAW LIMIT MARK

Place the block with the scroll end in the vice and saw the sides of the neck, stopping just short at the scroll. Do not free these, but handle the block with care to prevent the waste pieces catching and splitting off.

Turn the scroll sideways in the vice and cut the profile of the neck, pegbox and scroll. Cut these curves carefully, keeping as close to the lines as possible. Release the waste wood cut from the profile.

Take a chisel and file and, referring to the lines scribed on the side of the block, shave the work to the profile marks. Smooth the convex curves with the file, and then with straps of sandpaper backed by adhesive tape. Smooth the concavities with blocks or leather pads covered with sandpaper.

Once the profile of the neck and scroll are smooth and regular, and conform exactly to the template shape, cut below the scroll to release the side waste pieces. Take care not to cut

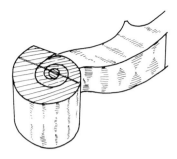

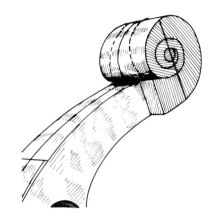

beyond them as it is easy to mark the side of the pegbox.

Use a marking gauge, dividers and a sheet of flexible, straight-sided cardboard to re-establish and mark the centreline of scroll, pegbox and neck. Use the cardboard to join the centre points once they have been established with the dividers and draw along its straight edge to link the marks.

With the centreline established, use dividers to mark off the widths for the pegbox and scroll. It will be seen from the photographs and plans that the width line is curved to give the scroll delicacy and grace. Join the divider marks using the straight-sided cardboard, taking the line round to the pegbox, but no further. Check the symmetry of the marks and adjust them for fairness.

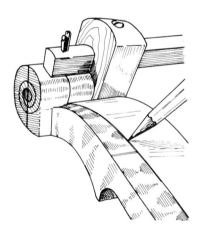

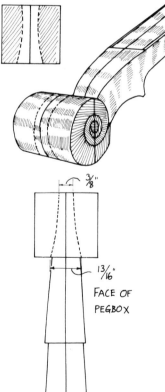

$\frac{3}{8}$"

$\frac{13}{16}$"

FACE OF PEGBOX

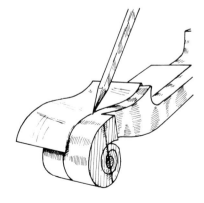

BACK OF
PEGBOX.

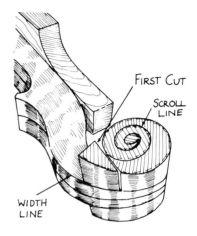

FIRST CUT

SCROLL
LINE

WIDTH
LINE

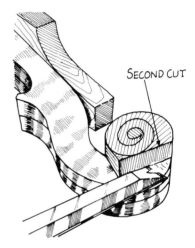

SECOND CUT

Take an offcut of hardwood for a neck support and shape it to resemble the illustration. It should be about ¾ in wider than the base of the neck; taper its top so that the neck, pegbox and scroll can be carved without the support in the way.

Fix the support to the neck using a short screw, which enters the neck just below the position for the top nut, and a longer screw at the base of the neck, just before the point at which it will be sawn off when fitted to the belly.

Place the neck in the vice with the side of the scroll uppermost and, with a backsaw, make a perpendicular cut into the side of the scroll until the saw reaches the width line on that side. Use a bevel-edged chisel to remove the waste and to smooth the side of the pegbox. Do not undercut.

Work a little further round the scroll and make a second cut, terminating the cut when the saw approaches the width line of the scroll. Release the waste as before. Continue with a third cut in a similar way and carry on cutting and clearing around the scroll until you reach

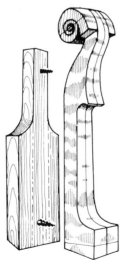

the point where there is no longer a pair of width marks for the saw to refer to. This is as far as this side can be cut, until the rise of the scroll is pencilled in. Turn the neck over and repeat on the other side. It is not important to reproduce the same sawcuts and angles, but it is vitally important not to stray inside any of the guidance marks or to undercut.

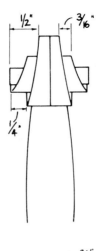

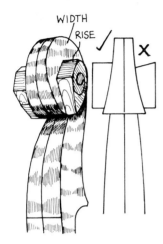

Turn the scroll back to its original side and use a bevel-edged chisel to cut away the corners between the saw cuts. Use the chisel to ease away all the waste wood on the waste side of the line, and to reveal the curl of the scroll still partly hidden in the wood. Do not undercut. It is sufficient to chop out the waste and to keep the width cut and the scroll cuts at right angles to each other. Once both sides of the scroll resemble the illustration below, refer to the plan

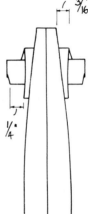

drawing of the scroll and note the rise of the scroll from the width line. Mark this at several points around the scroll with a pair of dividers. Then, with a pencil resting against a suitable sized piece of wood, draw round the rise,

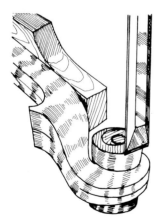

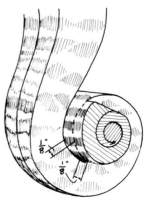

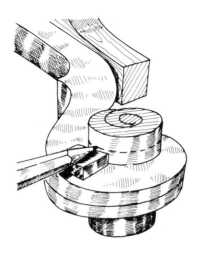

Errors at this point are usually caused by you being too timid in cutting to the width line, consequently throwing out the line marking the rise. Make the necessary alterations and then continue cutting and clearing around the curl of the scroll. Repeat on the other side but stop short before the centre of the scroll is reached. The final segment of the curl is best cut by chisel.

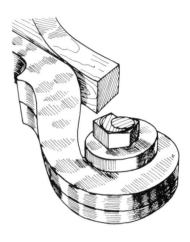

linking the marks. Repeat this on the opposite side of the scroll and then adjust the line so that it rises towards the tip of the eye in a simple sweeping curve. Repeat this on the other side and then inspect the neck and scroll from all angles to ensure the work so far is symmetrical.

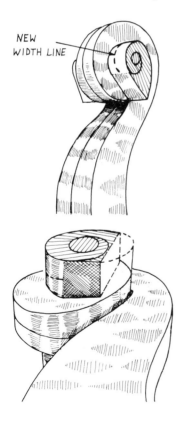

NEW
WIDTH LINE

Once this stage is reached it is time to take stock of the work so far, and to bring each side to the same degree of finish.

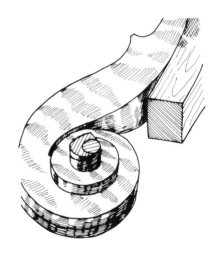

Take a file, and resting it on the width with its side against the rise of the scroll, file round the rise until it is a smooth spiral. Repeat on the other side and then mark around the edges of

Although you may possess a set of carving gouges which conform to the curves required for the release cut, it is a lot easier to use a very fine pointed scalpel to snip away the chips round the rise. Whichever tool is used, make certain that it does not undercut the rise. The eye forms what should seem to be a rod passing straight through the scroll. Undercutting the rise not only complicates the waste release cut, but adds nothing to the beauty of the work, while the maker who tries it runs the risk of losing his tight control over the carving.

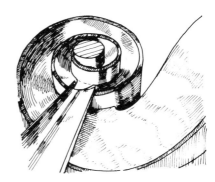

the scroll. Keep to the edge of the rise, and draw a ¹⁄₁₆ in thick line from the eye to the pegbox. Repeat on the other side.

Undercutting the scroll

This final stage brings life and grace to the carving. Instead of the width and rise being at right angles, the width is carved back and undercut as shown in the section through the scroll. You will see that there are two cuts needed to sink this depression – one to scoop out the depression and the other to release the waste.

Take a gouge of medium sweep and, with the scroll side up in the vice, carve from just inside the perimeter marks to just short of the eye. Use a scalpel to release the chip and repeat until the depth of the undercutting is reached.

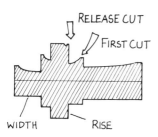

RELEASE CUT
FIRST CUT
WIDTH   RISE

Use a gouge to scoop out the depression – a flat gouge for that part adjacent to the pegbox and at the eye the smallest gouge. This is an easy cut, as by working downwards and inwards towards the eye the gouge is cutting with the grain. The release cut is more difficult as it must keep to the tight curve of the eye and not stray onto the surface of the width.

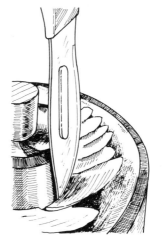

Work outwards from this cut, changing to a smaller diameter gouge as the curve of the scroll tightens, and to a larger, flatter gouge as the curve opens up. Do not overdo the under-cutting – it is the shadows which form in the recesses that give the scroll its beauty, and there is no need to dig away in order to achieve that lightness. Remember, too, that the outside of the scroll is also grooved, and these grooves raise the edges of the scroll to a fine, thin and sometimes vulnerable edge, requiring little in the way of tunnelling in the undercut to highlight their grace.

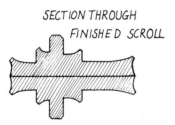

SECTION THROUGH
FINISHED SCROLL

Leave the final nick at the eye to the last. Once the first side is sunk and before it has been cleaned with the gouge and scrapers, turn over the scroll and repeat on the opposite side.

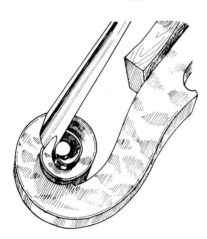

Turn again to the first side and, after adjusting the swing arm lamp to give a low light, use a gouge to remove the ridges between the initial sinking cuts in the spiral. With a little practice the steel of the gouge can be rested against the side of the eye to increase control of the sweep. Do not try to accomplish remodelling the spiral in this way. Obtain the overall shapes with the short cuts towards the centre of the scroll, and only trim them and level them with the sweep cuts.

As the spiral unwinds towards the pegbox, the sinking is reduced and the undercutting is less pronounced, until the width line sweeps round the last curve onto the flat side of the pegbox.

Once the gouge has removed the bumps and depressions in the carving, change to small scrapers, and lightly stroke these over the width cut of the spiral. Do not use the scrapers for altering the modelling of the scroll. Again, if remodelling is required, step back two stages, cut in, smooth off and then scrape again. Finish with a pad of fine 220 grit paper wrapped around a leather block that has its underside shaped to a curve.

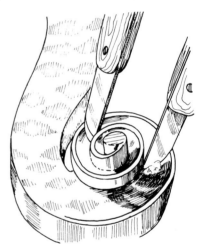

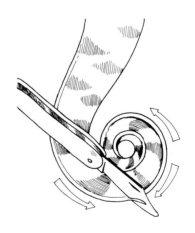

When both width cuts have been finished with sandpaper, take a knife, then a file or a block of wood with some sandpaper spray mounted to it and very lightly cut around the lip of the scroll, removing the pencil mark and smoothing minor bumps. This is an opportunity to work a fine bevel at the rim of the scroll but, bevelled or not, the face of the edge should be flat and clean.

Cutting the grooves on the outside of the scroll
The scroll carving is finished when the outer grooves are completed. The depth of these grooves can vary, dependent on the width of the scroll.

heel of the pegbox, and then with a small gouge or penknife begin to cut the groove at the crown of the scroll. Work the groove in both directions, cutting both sides in parallel, until it is roughed out over its full length except at the heel of the pegbox. These grooves are difficult to cut, partly because they lie across end grain and also because the right result is rather subtle. They need to look strong – cut too deep, and they become insubstantial. The best effects are achieved by deepening the grooves at their outer edges so that they strongly define the shape at the edge, without losing too much wood in the middle (see below).

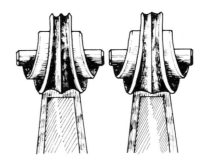

Mark a pencil line around the edge of the scroll and pegbox as illustrated to serve as a carving mark. Mark in the finished curve at the

Once there is the start of the groove around the outside of the scroll, cut across the depression, opening up the groove until it reaches both the centreline and the outer mark. Use the penknife and the small gouge to smooth away ridges in the carving. Take the grooves as far under the turn of the scroll as possible, consistent with clean workmanship. Smooth them with scrapers and sandpaper wrapped over shaped leather pads. Do not try

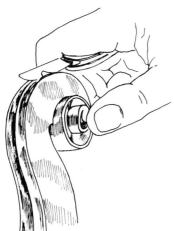

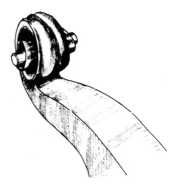

to finish the back of the pegbox at this stage, as it is almost certain to be damaged when the pegbox is hollowed.

Hollowing the pegbox

Remove the neck support. Mark off from the centreline the widths for the pegbox, referring to the illustration of the plan of the scroll and pegbox opposite. Note that the sides of the pegbox are thinner at the nut to give the strings

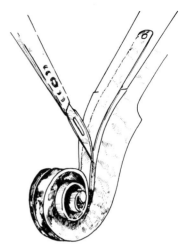

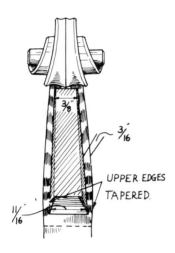

a clear run to the pegs. Support the scroll before chopping out the pegbox. If the waste sawn from the back of the neck is still available, cover its sawn face with a strip of felt and nestle the work back into its original block. If the waste is not available, it will be necessary to arrange other packing pieces which will take the force of the chopping and prevent the pegbox from snapping off.

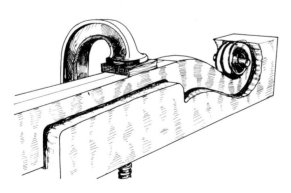

Once the neck is held and well supported, take a flexible steel ruler or a hacksaw blade and rest it along the line for the edges of the pegbox. Cut down the line with a scalpel. This should prevent the chisel from splitting out chips as the wood inside the marks is removed.

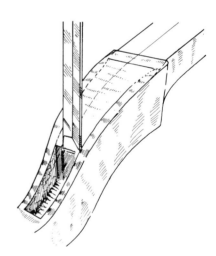

Take the ⅜ in bevel-edged chisel and a light mallet and, following in the sequence illustrated opposite, make a series of cuts into the face of the pegbox. Offset the chisel on alternate sides; if each cut is only a small distance behind the cut already made, the full width of the slot in the pegbox can be cut in one row of cuts. Stop just a little short of the line for the nut. Use the bevel-edged chisel gently. It is not designed for heavy work. Take small cuts,

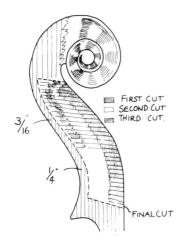

FIRST CUT
SECOND CUT
THIRD CUT.

3/16"

1/4"

FINAL CUT

Finishing the grooves
Refit the neck support and invert the scroll. Redefine the marks around the chin of the peg-box and from the chin carve the groove and fair it into the grooves sweeping down from the scroll. At the point where these two cuts meet there will be an area of neutral grain that can be worked in either direction, and this is probably the most difficult part to bring to a satisfactory

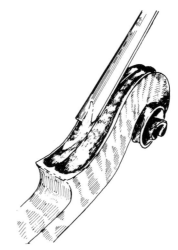

each cut removing a chip no larger than 1/16 in thick and 1/4 in deep. As the recess deepens check the vertical alignment of the chisel. It must not lean into the cut – to be safe, angle the handle slightly over the sides of the pegbox, so that the recess narrows slightly towards its base.

As the depth increases, measure the depth inside against the overall depth of the sides. For this, use a strip of lining or a length of dowel, using the thumb as a fence and stop. Leave a little over 1/4 in of wood at the base of the pegbox, and clean up its base, using the 3/8 in chisel. Trim the sides of the pegbox with a large flat chisel, then file and sand them smooth. Finish by cutting back to the end nut line.

finish. Work this area as best you can with a sharp gouge, then smooth it with some very sharp scrapers used lightly and at an angle to the grain. Follow with sandpaper wrapped around a leather strap.

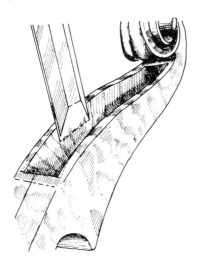

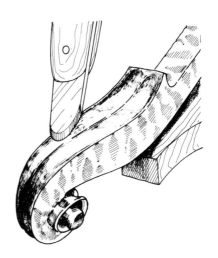

Final sanding

Once the scroll and pegbox is carved and sanded wash it in cold water and leave to dry. The water will clean the crevices in the scroll and also raise the grain of the wood. When it is dry take this opportunity to work over the scroll and pegbox with a scalpel, scraping away unevennesses and smoothing parts that had previously been missed. Do not press hard. Concentrate on cutting rather than depressing highspots and splinters. Any rough work at this stage will be revealed when the scroll and pegbox is washed a second time. Sand the surfaces to remove all of the rough grain, but take care to avoid sanding the corners and bevels, and the ridges between the two grooves running outside the scroll and pegbox. Sanding these features softens them, and the carving loses its definition. After this second thorough sanding, wash the work and leave it to dry. Provided that the work following the previous wash was light and incisive, the irregularities should be gone. When it is dry, lightly sand it smooth.

Repairing mistakes when carving the scroll

The most common mistake in carving the scroll is to remove too much wood from the sides of the curl during the initial shaping, as described on page 98. If this happens, repair the damage before proceeding rather than adapt the design to accommodate the new fault. The illustrations show typical errors. Where there is a small fault the situation is very straightforward, and a small strip of suitable wood can be glued into

the side of the curl and held with spring clamps; the marks are then redrawn to follow the shape of the existing spiral as illustrated. However, the larger the area of wood that has to be replaced, the more difficult it is to redraw the

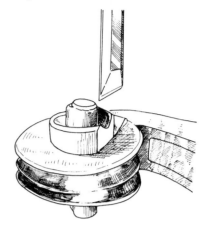

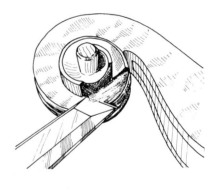

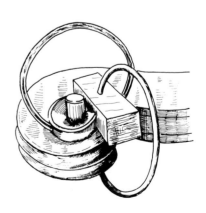

106

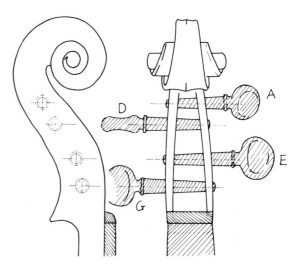

spiral accurately on the side of the scroll and the bigger the join that has to be disguised.

In the case of the illustration above the simplest and the quickest repair is to chisel off the entire side of the scroll and level it with a block plane, and then fit a new piece. The side

is then treated as though it is at the preliminary marking stage, except that the centrepoints for the eye will have to be worked from locating marks drawn on a face board, which allow the

eye position to be transferred from one side of the neck to the other, as illustrated. Fit the template as before and start cutting and carving as described on page 98.

Boring the pegholes
Bore the holes for the pegs while the neck is separate from the belly. The side elevation of the pegbox shows that the pegs are situated almost equidistantly and are positioned with the strings only touching the peg that they are fastened to. Notice, also, that each peg is canted so that the string tension draws the pegs harder into the cheeks of the pegbox.

The centrepoints for the pegholes are marked on the plans. If the pegbox accords to the plans, use them to transfer their position on one side of the box.

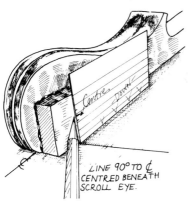

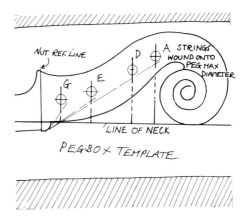

If there are no plans or template available, trace the outline of the pegbox and neck onto some paper (as described on page 41) and estimate the positions for the pegs. The only one which causes difficulty is the *D* peg, which is on the top left, facing the pegbox. Mark off the spacing of the pegs with the *A* and the *D* pegs being a little closer together than the *G* and *E* strings.

Extend the line of the neck with a straight-edge and then square off these lines down the sides of the pegbox. First mark in the position for the *A* string, which should be just below the turn of the scroll. The centrepoint should be a little towards the front of the pegbox. Use the centrepoint for the centre of a $3/16$ in diameter circle. Mark the position for the *E* string peg, closer to the back of the pegbox. Draw the $3/16$ in circle at its centrepoint. Mark in the *G* string peg, place it about equidistant from the front and back of the box. Draw the $3/16$ in diameter circle over this as well.

Draw in the top nut, and then a line from the top of each peg to the nut. With a compass set to $1/16$ in radius, find a point on the line for the *D* string where the arc of the peg is clear of the strings drawn to the top of the *A* peg, and where a line drawn from the *D* peg does not touch the top of the *E* peg. By adjusting the positions for the *A* and *E* pegs, room should be made for the *D*. Mark in the centrepoint for the *D* and prepare to transfer these marks to the pegbox.

From the drawing mark off the position of each peg on the side of the filing card. Mark the position of the nut, and the four pegs along one edge, and their height above the neck base line on another.

With the neck face down on the drawing, mark off the longitudinal position of each peg. Then, using the height marks, slide the card to each line, and mark in the line and centrespot for each peg.

At this stage, whether or not a template has been used, the marks will be on one side only of the pegbox, each centrepoint intersected by a perpendicular line to the front of the pegbox.

Although it is possible to work the slight cant of the pegs once a hole, square to the centre-lines, has been drilled, it is better to complete the careful marking work at this stage, rather than rely on working the cant by eye with the reamer.

The centreline of the neck should be clearly visible. Take a sheet of clean typing paper, and fold it down the middle, aligning the edges and corners accurately. Harden the crease with your thumb nail and then snick two diamonds from the centreline. Open out the typing paper.

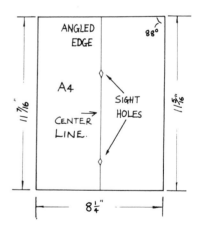

Mark the cant for the pegs on the top of the paper, using the angle and dimensions suggested in the illustration, and with the centreline of the paper directly over the line on the neck, and with the cant sloping downwards towards the left, mark across the pegbox the line for the *E* and *A* strings.

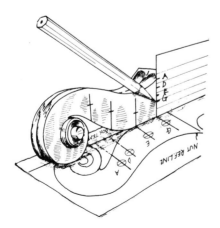

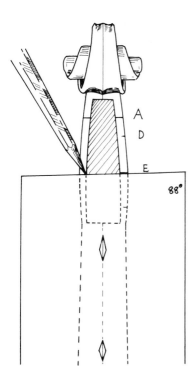

Once these lines have been drawn across the edges of the pegbox and onto the second face side, turn the neck face downwards again. With the filing card used before, mark on the perpendiculars, and the centrepoint for each peg.

Use a ³⁄₁₆ in diameter drill for the pegholes. Refix the neck to the neck support which was used for carving. Hold a block of wood inside the pegbox to arrest the movement of the drill once it has cut through the first side. With the neck lying horizontally in the vice, drill down each peghole, turn the neck over and drill the other side. Complete the final stages of reaming the holes when the neck is fitted and the instrument is varnished.

Reverse the paper, so that the card slopes to the right, and mark in the *G* and *D* strings. Note that on the second side, the original marks on the pegbox indicate the position for the centre of the peg drilled perpendicular to the centre-line. Since there is a slight cant, keep the lines just short of the marks for the second side (as illustrated).

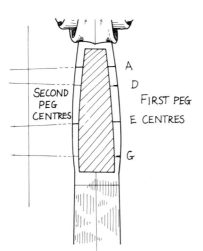

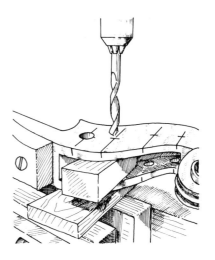

Fitting and trimming the neck

One of the last phases in making a violin is to join the neck to the body of the instrument. Both components represent a considerable investment in skill and dedication. The prospect of joining them, in perfect alignment and at the correct angle, where there are so few clear reference marks to work to, may seem daunting.

However, the neck joint is simple, and if it is cut in sequence, the corrections for the alignment etc., can be made well before the joint is close to being finished. The illustrations below specify the three elements which must be checked during the fitting of the neck.

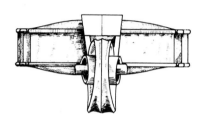

a

Illustration a shows the instrument seen from the top. The scroll must be square with the sides, back and front of the instrument. It is easy to inadvertently introduce a twist between the neck and the body and equally easy to avoid it if frequent checks from this angle are made.

Illustration b shows the perfect alignment of the neck with the centreline of the instrument. When cutting to length, this is the first element in the fitting to be accomplished, and although it is unlikely to change, this, too, must be checked constantly.

Illustration c shows the profile of the finished instrument. The correct angle for the neck can be calculated from a profile drawing. Note that the eyes of the scroll touch a line extended from the back to the side join. A line from the face of the neck, extended to the bottom of the instrument, will be just a little over the height of the sides above the belly.

Cutting the heel

If the instrument is made according to the plans, the length of the neck and the angle at which it should bear against the end block can be lifted straight from the drawings, and you can move to the section entitled *Marking and cutting the neck joint*.

Finding the correct angle for the neck

Draw the full-size dimensions of the violin in profile on a large sheet of cardboard. As well as marking in its length, depth and the height of

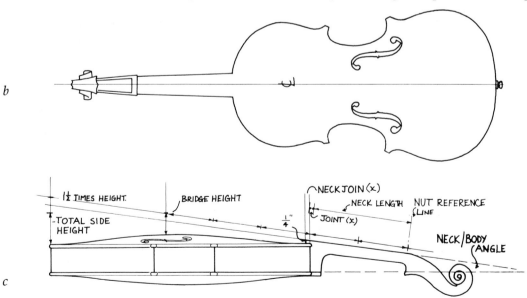

b

c

the belly arching, also mark the position of the f holes relative to the ends of the instrument. The drawing should resemble *illustration c*. The mid-point of the f holes should straddle the strongest part of the bass bar on which the bridge stands; this gives us the position for the bridge.

Extend vertical lines from each end. At the base, mark up the height of the sides, and at the neck join, mark off a point ¼ in above the belly. Take a straightedge, and from a point just slightly above the top mark on the base line at the bottom of the instrument, draw a line through the height mark above the belly towards the scroll. The angle made between this line and the vertical at the neck of the instrument is the correct neck/body angle.

The neck length is calculated using the same profile drawing. Draw in a 1³⁄₁₆ in vertical line to represent the bridge. Mark off, on the vertical base line, a point 1½ times the height of the sides. Mark off on the vertical line at the neck joint a string mark, ½ in above the surface of the belly. This represents the position of the string over the fingerboard at this point. Draw a line through these points, marking the top of the bridge, and carry the line straight down to the scroll.

The Rule of 5 described on page 73 can now be applied to calculate the length of the neck. Divide the line from the top of the bridge to the string mark at the neck into three. Set a pair of dividers to this one third measurement, and mark off two more thirds for the neck. This will

be the position for the nut reference line. Add to this length the depth of the slot sunk into the end block, then draw in the cutting line for the neck.

Marking and cutting the neck joint

With the length of the neck accurately established, and using the square end of the template that had been used for marking the peg positions, square across the face of the neck. Align the diamond marks on the centre-line, cut into the face of the neck and mark along the square edge of the paper. When the line has been pencilled in, go over the line with a marking knife and straightedge.

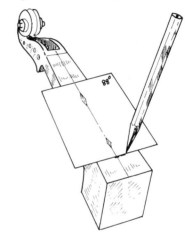

Take the angle for the neck from the drawing, with an angle bevel or with a filing card. When the angle is marked on both sides, place the

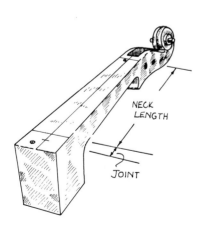

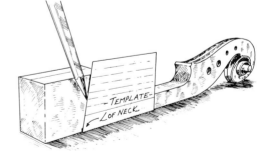

neck in the bench hook, relieve the waste side with a chisel, and saw off the waste with a backsaw.

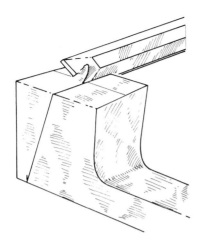

neck can be made by planing the face of the neck, but before doing so, ensure that the centrelines on the neck and heel are carefully scribed onto the end grain of the heel and the pegbox, so that they can be re-established later. When the twist for the neck has been checked, and new marks have been made, cut away the small section of belly that covers the top of the neck joint. This is cut well inside the lines with a knife, and trimmed back with a file until the edge of the belly is perfectly flush with the slot.

Draw a line to connect the centrelines on the top and the bottom of the neck. Mark in a vertical down the middle of a filing card, and pin this vertical to the sawn face of the neck to check for twist.

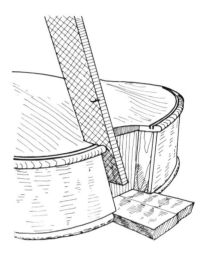

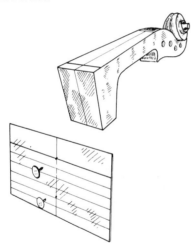

Take the original template or an offcut of card and, with a knife and straightedge, trim the shape until it fits perfectly into the slot at the top of the instrument. Mark on it the centrelines from the line drawn up the middle of the slot.

Sight down the scroll. It should line up with the face of the neck, and the horizontal lines on the card. Minor adjustments to a twist in the

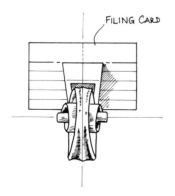

FILING CARD

At the heel, draw across the height line, which marks the upper edge of the belly where the heel enters the slot in the body of the violin. Pin the slot template with its outer face pressed against the sawn face of the heel, position it just below the height line and exactly on the centre-line. Draw down both edges of the template before removing it.

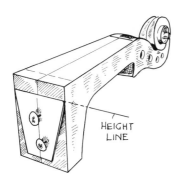

Place the neck in the bench hook and use a chisel to cut close to the two lines marked on the end of the neck. Slot the neck into place. Systematically check the three components that determine its correct alignment. If the neck is tilted off the centreline, shave down the bearing face of the neck. If it is twisted, adjust the two side cuts to correct the twist; if the angle of the neck is wrong, adjust the pitch of the front face.

As the fitting progresses, the neck will slip closer to the button at the back of the violin. These adjustments become critical as the height line at the front edge of the neck approaches the surface of the belly, but by this stage adjustments should be confined to preventing any

twist from being introduced into the neck as the sides are shaved down.

As the height line approaches the top of the belly, mark the high points of the heel and shave these away. Finish fitting the neck with chalk, trimming the sides with a file and the heel with a block plane. Once it is in place, check the angles, alignment and twist of the neck. Small alterations are still possible, but at the cost of going beyond the height line or packing the joint.

When the neck is fitting well, pencil round the sides of the heel to mark the depth of the slot and then remove the neck for reinforcement and shaping.

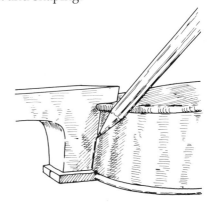

Reinforcing the neck

A reinforcing slip of wood inserted vertically into the neck, across the short grain of the heel, adds strength to this joint. Although it is rare for a violin neck to split across the short grain of

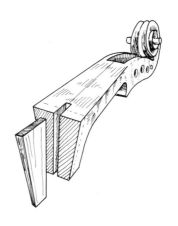

the heel, it does happen and is quite a common occurrence in cellos.

Mark the centreline on the joining face of the heel. Measure in ¼ in at the base of the heel, and ⅝ in at the top face. Draw in two lines, one each side of the centreline ¹⁄₁₆ in apart. Cut down the line with a backsaw, stopping at the marks on the heel and the neck. Saw the second line parallel to the first. Remove the waste with the purfling chisel.

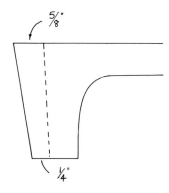

Select a slip of straight-grained hardwood, true one edge, and plane it until it slides easily into the slot. If the reinforcing slip rocks, shave away its inner face until it fits steadily in the slot. Size the slip and apply thick hide glue to the slot before sliding the reinforcement piece quickly into position.

When the glue has hardened, saw the slip and pare away its prominent edge on the glueing face with a chisel. The reinforcing piece will have to be sunk slightly to accommodate the different rates of shrinkage between the end grain of the reinforcement slip and the short grain of the heel, which would otherwise leave

the end of the reinforcement strip proud of the face of the neck and lever off the fingerboard.

Gouge a shallow depression along the ends of the reinforcing piece and up the joining face of the neck. This joining face helps air and excess glue to escape when fitting the neck.

Shaping the neck

Screw the neck to the neck support and place it horizontally in the vice. With the cardboard straightedge, mark a centreline down the back of the neck, lining it up with the centreline and reinforcing slip on the heel and the centre ridge of the pegbox.

Draw the shape for the button. This must be symmetrical, but its actual shape is a matter of preference. Avoid a perfect semi-circle, which would seem inappropriate in an instrument that eschews hard predictable shapes. Err on the large side, and draw in a slightly flattened curve, echoing the curves of the instrument and resembling, if anything, a contented cat curled up at the top of the back.

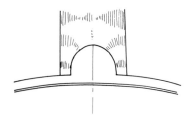

Draw in the curve at the chin of the pegbox and then carve the neck in the following way.

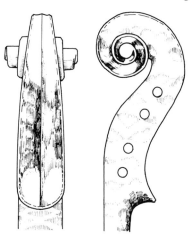

With a flat chisel, work a bevel down the sides of the heel and along the neck, finishing with cuts to the neck and chin. Cut a second and then third bevel around the neck and continue until the roughing in is complete.

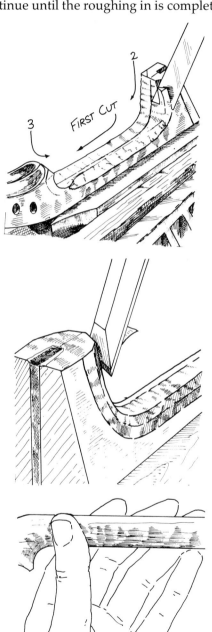

This is the point at which the neck should be taken from the neck support and held between the thumb and first finger, where it should rest easily. If the instrument is being made for a child, for instance, or a player with small hands, cut back the neck even more, until it resembles a curved V section. Follow the sizes in the drawing below, before commencing to smooth the neck.

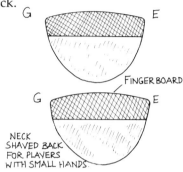

Finishing the neck

Once the overall shape and section for the neck have been defined by the preliminary bevelling, pare away the corners of the bevels with a sharp chisel until the neck is nicely rounded. Take a knife and flat gouge and repeat on the neck and chin of the pegbox, making sure that you test and feel for irregularities and unevennesses. Take care never to stray beyond the marks which delineate the start of the neck/body join, or to cut too deeply into the change of curve at the heel and chin. This area should be the last to be brought to its correct line and finished shape. Scrape and sand the neck, chin and heel smooth.

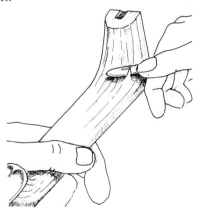

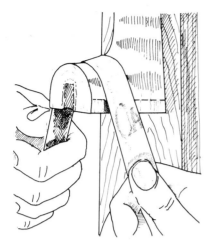

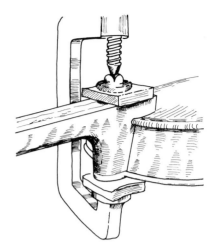

Slip the neck into the slot in the instrument and draw round the base of the heel onto the rough-cut button. Cut the button to its approximate shape with a scroll saw.

pads and a C-clamp over the button, with a leather pad between the neck and the clamp. Tighten the clamp. Wash away surplus glue with clean hot water and wipe dry.

Trimming the button

When the glue is dry, remove the clamps and with a sharp chisel carve away the rough edges of the button, stopping just short of the edges of the back. Finish the shaping with files and sandpaper, and then trim round the edge of the back to the button with a chisel. Clean up the button and finish this completely before rounding off the remaining fraction of the unfinished edge.

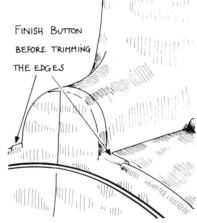

FINISH BUTTON BEFORE TRIMMING THE EDGES

Joining the neck

Check all around for misalignments and irregularities and correct where necessary before removing the neck and sizing both faces of the joint in preparation for glueing. Wipe away the excess glue and collect two leather pads, a wooden block to press against the button, and a small C-clamp.

Apply glue to both surfaces and and slip and press the neck into position. Quickly fit the

Work over the neck, heel and chin with scrapers and then sandpaper backed by leather pads, until it is smooth and perfectly formed.

Fitting up

The end rest

The end rest is fitted once the instrument is assembled. It straddles the centreline at the bottom of the violin with its raised edge lifting the tail gut above the belly.

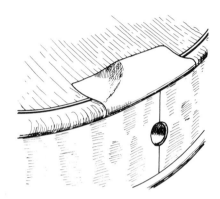

An end rest can be easily fashioned from a length of ebony piano key or offcut of boxwood. Square the face of the rest and saw and smooth the end cuts to a slight bevel. Cut a front bevel for the rest, stopping the bevel at the height line of the belly. Hold the rest in position, centring it over the join of the lower bouts and the centre-line of the belly. Mark round its front and side faces with a scalpel.

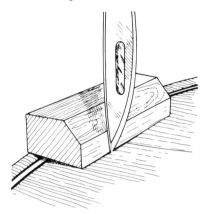

Remove the rest and, working well inside the lines in the belly, cut away the waste wood with a scalpel to expose the end block. Once the bulk of the wood is removed, work to the line with a bevel-edged chisel.

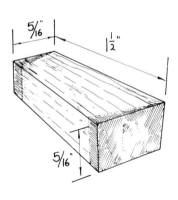

BELLY THICKNESS

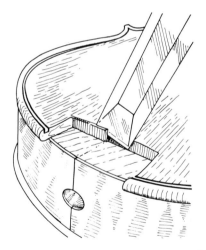

Slip the end rest into position. It should be a perfect fit. If it is a little loose shave away the front face. This widens the fitting to make an easy press fit. Size the slot and apply glue to both joining faces. Press the end rest into place. Wash away surplus glue with clean hot water, and leave the glue to harden.

117

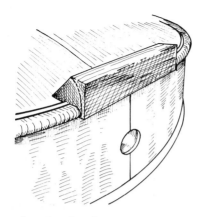

Once the glue has hardened, use a plane or file to smooth the outer edges of the rest. Use a penknife to cut the two small cuts which curve

from the bearing edge of the end rest to the surface of the belly. Take a chisel and round the back edge of the rest to remove any hard edges, then finish with a file and sandpaper.

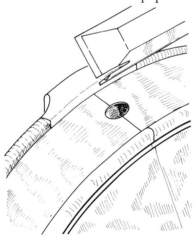

Apart from setting up and varnishing, the violin is now finished. The reader will know that there is a lot left to do, but tackled systematically and excluding drying time, most of the work can be fitted into one full working day. The varnish has to cover the entire body of the instrument, including the area of belly obscured by the fingerboard, but because fitting the fingerboard often necessitates minor reshaping of the neck and heel, it is worthwhile fitting the fingerboard temporarily, then removing it and varnishing the instrument when the alterations to the neck have been made.

The pegs, fingerboard, tailpiece, etc, which are needed for fitting out the violin, can all be bought from mail order firms specializing in supplying instrument makers and it is recommended that ready-made good quality ebony fittings are used.

Once the fittings are at hand, the first step is to fit the fingerboard and top nut, before varnishing the instrument.

The fingerboard

Lighten the neck before the fingerboard is fitted. Take a small gouge and hollow the part of the neck between the nut and the reinforcement. Leave a ¼ in margin at the sides of the neck, and stop the gouging before the nut. Run the gouge lines out over the reinforcement piece. Take the block plane, set it to a very fine cut and smooth and level the surface of the neck. Take two pins and tap them into the nut

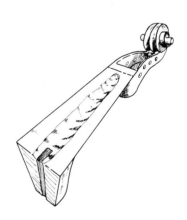

line to provide a location for the end of the fingerboard when it is slid into position. Take the fingerboard and look at its edges. They are likely to be thicker than is desirable and will need to be shaved down: 3/16 in or slightly less is a satisfactory thickness. Before thinning the fingerboard, place it on the neck, and measure off the height of the upper edge of the fingerboard end from the belly. The measurement should be about one inch to the belly, and 1½ in at the bridge. If the measurements are less than this, bevel the underside of the fingerboard to lift it slightly.

You will see that, quite apart from the obvious curve of the section of the fingerboard, the face is concave in the longitudinal plane. This, with the taper, makes the fingerboard a difficult item to clamp.

Take a pine board and carve in it a depression into which the fingerboard will rest. With the board held in the vice, lightly plane the underside of the fingerboard, making adjustments to the angle where necessary. Refit the fingerboard and chalk it down to obtain a perfect fit.

Once the fit is obtained and the angle of the fingerboard is correct, remove it and mark in the area immediately above the hollowing in the neck. Gouge out a small depression in the fingerboard to remove unnecessary weight. Test the squareness of the top against the nut line and also mark in the centrepoint of the fingerboard at its ends.

Replace the fingerboard, and check it for a level fit. At this stage the edges of the fingerboard are likely to overhang the sides of the neck and it is also probably too long.

Cut a slip of newspaper the size of the fingerboard, and glue this to the face of the neck. This will ease its removal later. Then, locating the fingerboard with the pins stuck in the neck, apply more thinned glue to the neck, and press the fingerboard in place, clamping it with two spring hand clamps, with leather pads beneath their jaws. Before leaving it to dry, check the fingerboard is in its correct alignment and is overhanging equally on each side. As soon as the glue has chilled, clean the glue residue from the top of the fingerboard, and slip the end nut

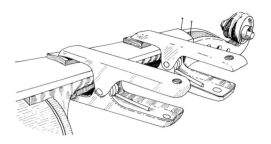

into position. Trim it until it fits neatly into the recess with its upper face leading into the slope of the end of the pegbox. Once a satisfactory fit is obtained, glue a small slip of newspaper on the neck above the fingerboard, glue the nut to it and leave it to harden.

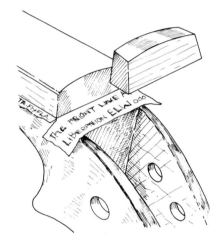

When the glue is dry, take a knife and delicately whittle away at the edges of the

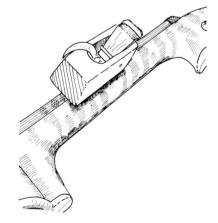

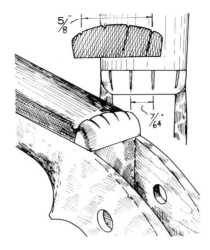

fingerboard until they lie flush with the sides of the neck. Take a small plane or a file and smooth the edges to the very ends of the fingerboard. File off the overhangs on the nut and roughly shape it to follow the curve of the fingerboard about 1/32 in higher than its surface. Mark off the correct length of the fingerboard which should terminate just below the corners of the upper bout. Mark this line across the fingerboard, using the cardboard straightedge. Remove the fingerboard with a thin steel kitchen knife, and cut the fingerboard to length.

File the end flat and shave the underside of the end with a penknife to present a finer edge than at the sides. Store the fingerboard with the other ebony fittings where they will remain undamaged. Trim a small thin piece of scrapwood to the shape of the fingerboard and tape

it to the neck with brown gummed tape to protect the neck edges while it is varnished. (See *Varnishing* on page 200.)

Fitting up the instrument after varnishing
Clean up the glueing faces of the fingerboard and nut, which should still be fastened together. Clean the neck and place the two together. They should fit perfectly. If necessary shave the surfaces of the fingerboard and neck and chalk them together as described on page 43.

Size the fingerboard and, with slightly thinner glue than usual, apply glue to both surfaces. Slide the fingerboard into place. Align it and promptly grip the neck and the fingerboard together with two hand grips. Protect the neck and fingerboard with some leather strips between the jaws and the wood. Wash off surplus glue with hot water and poke a piece of wire into the hole between the fingerboard and the end of the neck to clear away any glue that might be blocking it. When the glue is dry, scrape round the edges of the neck and if necessary adjust the size and shape of the neck before finishing with fine sandpaper backed by a leather pad.

Use a file to remove bumps and sharp edges from the nut, and smooth it with fine sandpaper, taking care to avoid over-running and rounding the edges of the pegbox adjacent to it. Use the pattern above to mark the string grooves which are cut in the nut with the tip of a rat-tailed file.

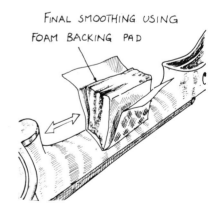

FINAL SMOOTHING USING FOAM BACKING PAD

Finish by sanding the face and side of the fingerboard and the back of the neck, using strips of sandpaper backed by brown plastic adhesive tape and then fine paper backed by a firm foam pad. Refinish the neck using a hard quick-drying varnish or shellac polish.

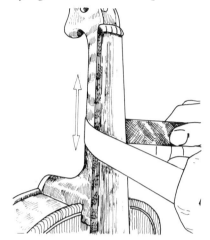

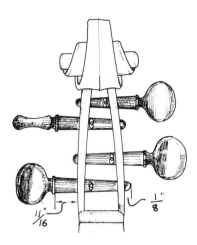

The tail pin

The tapered tail pin is fitted into a hole in the bottom block of the instrument. This has already been drilled, but still needs to be reamed out. Check the cutters of the reamer to make sure they are sharp and free from compacted sawdust. If the cutters are blunt, hone them with a fine Arkansas stone as illustrated earlier. Fit the handle and start the point into the hole in the end block and turn it gently. As the reamer revolves in the hole, the cutters enlarge it to the desired size and taper. Use this brief operation to gain a feel for the reamer before cutting the pegholes. The tail pin should fit easily into the hole at the base of the instrument. Keep pressure at a minimum and the tool steady to prevent tearing the wood. Test the fit of the tail pin until it slides into the end block.

The pegs

The correct fitting for the pegs is shown in the illustration following. Note the cant of the pegs into the pegbox and also the regular distance between the cheeks of the pegbox and the shoulders of the pegs. Each peg should fit tightly into both sides of the pegbox.

Before the pegs are fitted, the holes in the pegbox will have to be reamed. It is easier to control the alignment of the pegs if each peg hole is reamed and its peg fitted individually. Reference has already been made to the cant of the pegs as they enter the pegbox, the angle causing the pegs to be drawn into the box by the tension of the strings. Apart from this slight cant, the peg must be perfectly square with the major planes of the instrument. Thus, seen from the head of the scroll, every peg should be parallel and in line with the joint face of the belly and sides. Apart from checking the cant, the second and equally important check, as reaming is in progress, is to monitor their level and alignment. Before reaming, take four pieces of dowel and stick one through each pair of holes. Sight down the instrument. The dowels may reveal misalignments, which will have to be corrected by the reamer.

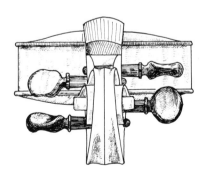

Draw a sketch, noting the misalignments for reference when reaming. The *G* string peg requires the least filing to fit and is therefore the one to do first. If it is left until last, and accidentally filed too small, none of the other pegs already fitted could substitute. Ream the hole carefully, making regular checks to the angle of the reamer to ensure it is bored at right angles to the face of the pegbox and at the cant illustrated. To adjust the angle add a slight sideways pressure to the handle of the tool. If a greater adjustment is needed, insert the tip of a nail into the recess at the end of the reamer, and apply gentle sideways pressure both at the handle and at the tip. Stop reaming when the tip has emerged from the opposite side of the pegbox, leaving a hole about $3/16$ in diameter.

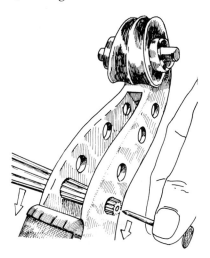

Make a simple jig to hold the pegs while you file and saw them. Use any suitable offcut of hard- or softwood. Mark a line across the face of the woodblock for the peg groove and leave room elsewhere on the block for a clamp with which to hold the block to the bench.

Saw down the line to a depth of $1/8$ in, then pare away the sides to make a V shaped groove with a bevel-edged chisel. Mark off and saw a slot across the groove one inch in from the end of the block, as illustrated. This sawcut is to guide the backsaw while it trims the ends of the pegs. It need not be deeper than the V cut.

Take one of the four ebony pegs and poke it in the reamed hole. It is unlikely to fit.

Remember that the finger grip should not fit hard against the sides of the pegbox, but should remain about $3/4$ in from the pegbox cheeks, with the tip of the peg protruding about $1/8$ in on the opposite side.

Place the peg in the block, with the finger grip hanging over the edge. Take a rough flat file and, with regular firm strokes, file a bevel on the shank to conform to the taper of the reamer. Turn the peg round and repeat until a new taper is made at its end. Try the fit repeatedly and adjust the taper until the peg emerges from the opposite side of the pegbox. Continue working the bevel further up the shaft, testing regularly to ensure that the peg is round and that both cheeks of the pegbox are gripping the peg. Once there is enough emerging peg to hold, grip the peg and try to rock it in the hole to see if it is loose. By this time, the fit should be good. Take a fine file and work over the shank, rounding and smoothing and testing. As the peg begins to emerge from the pegbox, both the taper and its roundness become increasingly important. To help achieve the correct fit, twist and press the peg in the hole before withdrawing it for filing. The burnish on the face of the peg indicates the parts which are tight. File these down in order to bring the low spots in contact with the cheeks of the pegbox.

By the time that the peg is fitted and the shaft passes through the pegbox with the finger grip ferrule about $3/4$ in away from the cheeks, the peg should be round, smooth and a good fit. If for some reason, the fitting has been a failure, and the peg, though penetrating the correct distance, is not a tight fit in both cheeks, relegate it to one of the other pegholes further up the box, which still have not been reamed.

With the peg fitted, take a pencil, lean the shank of the pencil against the side of the pegbox and draw a line onto the tip of the peg. This marks the sawing line. Place the peg in the V blocks, and align the pencil mark with the saw slot. Saw off the end of the peg with the backsaw. Bevel this end with a penknife, then round it by holding some 150 grit paper in the palm of the hand, and rub the sides and end until it is smooth and rounded. Burnish the rest of the peg shaft by placing the handle grip lightly in the vice, then rub a belt of cloth around the shaft to polish it.

Insert the peg and mark it where the inside face of the cheek is closest to the finger grip. The hole for the string will be drilled a short distance from this point. Remove the peg and place it in the V block and with a round rat-tailed file make a small groove 1/8 in down the shaft from the cheek mark. Bore a 1/16 in hole for the string. Make a second groove across the shaft where the hole emerges on the other side.

Fit each peg in turn and make frequent checks for alignment when boring the tapers and for roundness when filing the pegs to fit the taper.

When all four of the pegs have been fitted, check each peg to find if there is sufficient clearance between the peg and the pegbox for the strings. Take a spare D or G string, and wind it onto each peg in turn. Then if, after winding on five turns (including a double layer), there is

a danger that the peg will jam and break the sides of the pegbox, take a small flat chisel and shave away the base of the pegbox directly beneath the peg. Check thicknesses to ensure that the chisel does not break through the back of the pegbox. If, despite your best efforts, some pegs are a little too tight, or loose, take some Plasticine (modelling clay), warm it until it is soft, and insert a smudge of Plasticine into each peghole. Replace the pegs and twist them. The Plasticine lubricates and holds the pegs and adds a firm smoothness to their action.

The tail gut
Synthetic tail guts are available which allow rapid fitting and precise adjustment. The length of the gut is altered by turning the nuts threaded onto each end of the tail gut. These should be adjusted until the tailpiece is suspended by the strings and the gut a fraction above the endrest, as illustrated.

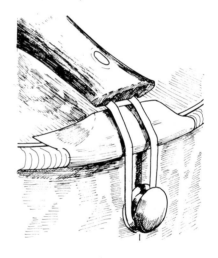

Fitting an organic tail gut is a lengthier, but simple enough process. The gut is obtained coiled a little longer than required for the violin. Take one end and hold it into a candle flame until it softens and swells. Press the end with the thumbnail to burr its top. Take some thick thread and tie a number of tight thumb knots at the end of the gut as illustrated. Push the other end of the gut through one of the two holes in the underside of the tailpiece and pull it through, leaving the thickened end stopped

inside the tailpiece. Bend the gut round the tail pin and back through the second hole in the tailpiece. Mark its correct position at the point of the tailpiece where the gut passes beneath its end. Remove the tailpiece from the violin and

cut away excess gut, leaving slightly more on the inside than is required for the burr. Burr and bind the second end. Shorten the gut by adding more thumb knots.

The soundpost

The diagram below shows the correct position for the soundpost. Alterations of position change the tone and response of the instrument. The diagrams show how, by moving the post sideways, different strings are favoured. Unresponsive instruments and those with high arching are enhanced by moving the soundpost closer to the bridge; flatter and more responsive fiddles produce a better tone if the post is moved further back. Note from the section through the instrument that the post is virtually beneath the right foot of the bridge and is perpendicular.

Make the soundpost from straight, close-grained pine. Its diameter should be about ¼ in. A thinner post favours higher notes. The line of its end grain should be at 90 degrees to the grain of the belly, which not only optimizes its contribution to the tone of the instrument, but is also the most convenient alignment for the fitting.

Select a suitable piece of timber about 4 in long for the soundpost. Split it roughly to size, and use a chisel and plane to work it into a perfect rod. When handling work as small as

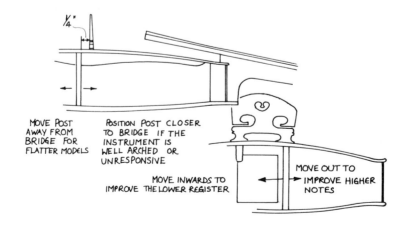

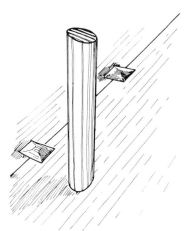

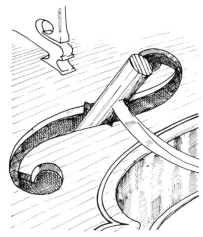

this, it is often a help to clamp the plane upside down in the vice and to move the wood over its face.

Hold the violin in both hands and sight down the back from the end pin, to obtain a clear view of its arching. The bottom and top of the soundpost must conform to the arching in order for the post to sit squarely on the back and belly. Study the angle between a vertical drawn from the foot of the bridge to the curve of the back. With the soundpost positioned and the grain aligned correctly, saw this angle at its foot and file the end smooth.

Lay the violin on its back and pass the post through its upper lobe of the right f hole. Hold it upright against the back of the instrument. Draw round the post at the f hole to mark in the level and curve of the belly. Withdraw the post and saw the top end. File the end smooth and mark its top for identification.

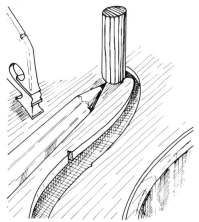

Take the soundpost setter and impale it in the post about ⅝ in from its top. Remove the tail piece and tailpin. Slide the post into the belly of the instrument through the f hole. Position the post by touching it down onto the inside back of the violin. Keeping the post perpendicular, pull its top towards you. As the post slips sideways it will catch against the roof of the belly and release the setter.

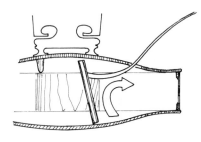

Sight down the tailpin hole to check its verticality. It should line up with the side of the top block. Adjust the post, using the hooks at the other end of the setter. Do not force it into position, but if it feels about to topple, apply light downwards pressure on the belly to steady it until it is pulled into place.

Once the post is in place, peer through the tailpin hole to see whether it is properly seated. Take it out and adjust it until it is in full contact with the back and belly. Remove the soundpost by knocking it down with the setter and then spearing it with a pin set in the end of a thin dowel or with a steel knitting needle, sharpened to a fine point.

Trim the ends, rub a little chalk on to them and replace the post. The post can be moved longitudinally once it is in position by tapping it with the hooked end of the setter.

The bridge

The bridge is fitted across the belly with its back face perpendicular to the surface of the belly at the mid-point of the f holes.

Take the bridge, place it in position, and draw around its feet, marking the curve of the belly with a sharp pencil. Remove the bridge and carve to the line with a penknife or chisel. Place a sheet of 220 grit paper on the belly, grit face up, and holding the bridge vertically over the paper rub it back and forth along the centreline of the belly. There should be no sideways, only longitudinal movement, and this restricted to about ⅜ in. Take great care to keep the bridge in its correct attitude to the belly and in its correct situation straddling the centreline. Fitting a bridge is a skilled task, as its feet must be in perfect contact over the surface of the belly. It helps to use the wheeled holder available from the mail order suppliers listed at the back of the book. Brace the bridge against the wheeled block, which automatically gives a vertical alignment.

The most common difficulty experienced by those who are trying to fit the bridge is that the feet are quite easily shaped to fit the curve of the belly, but an additional curve is introduced which causes it to rock. Once it is established, this curve is difficult to eliminate, unless the feet are taken back a stage and scraped with a knife until they are slightly hollowed on the underside. Return the bridge to the sandpaper and after a few firm finishing scrapes over the paper it should fit.

Take a straightedge and place it on the nut and bridge. The gap between the tip of the fingerboard and the straightedge is slightly more than ¹⁄₁₆ in for the E string, and a little more than ⅛ in for the G string. Estimate at the bridge the amount of correction required and remove the bridge and mark on its leading face the curve illustrated.

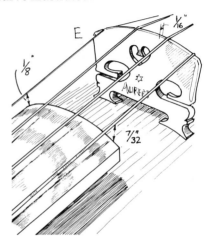

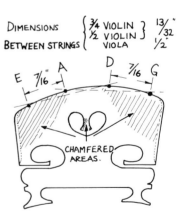

DIMENSIONS	¾ VIOLIN	¹³⁄₃₂"
BETWEEN STRINGS	½ VIOLIN	½"
	VIOLA	

Trim the bridge to the line and mark in the nicks for the strings. Cut the nicks and slip the bridge into place. String up the instrument and, after checking that the bridge is vertical and standing in the correct position defined by the small nicks in the f holes, sight across the strings. The A string should be one string

126

diameter above the tops of the *D* and *E*, and the *D* should be one diameter above the *G* and *A*. Remove the bridge and adjust until this is achieved; then hold the bridge over some sandpaper and lightly rock its edge until the curve is clean and smooth.

Once the bridge is fitted and the string nicks are set at the correct height and the right distance apart, trim the corners and bevel the edges of the bridge as illustrated; rub the tip of a lead pencil into each nick before fitting the strings. The fitting, height, thickness and position of the bridge subtly affect the instrument's tone. If the bridge is thin, the upper notes will be enhanced. A thicker bridge softens a hard tone.

Adjustments
Once the bridge is fitted, wind the strings onto the pegs in the manner illustrated, and tune the instrument. Always buy good quality strings as these will do justice to the instrument. The strings of a violin are tuned to *G, D, A, E*. As they reach pitch, the bridge will tilt forward. Correct this by holding its top edge just below the strings and heave it back vertical. New strings stretch slightly and frequent adjustments are needed for the first hour.

This is the time to rejoice in the creation of a new instrument, but also a time to be critical. At this stage it is the sound that is the main concern. Buzzes usually indicate either a loose

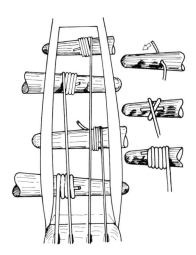

fitting such as a string adjustor which needs screwing tight or a strand of the tail gut which is pressing against the belly; or that the back or belly is not properly glued to the sides of the instrument. The tone should be of similar quality and responsiveness throughout its range, right up each string. To achieve this may mean experimenting with the position of the soundpost, moving it towards the centre to improve its lower register, or to the f holes for the upper notes.

You may notice that certain notes, especially in the higher registers, do not sound as well as others, almost as if there is a constriction in the instrument strangling a particular note, even though, at an octave lower, the same note is particularly strong. This suggests that the instrument, like many others, has a wolf note. Shortening the tail gut, moving the bridge, altering the bass bar, or thinning the belly may eliminate or suppress it. There are many variables that can be altered in order to achieve the best tone, and it is best to make as many experiments as soon as possible and then leave the instrument set up, preferably in a room where music is played regularly, so that it can settle into its adjustment.

Friends and relatives are likely to be impressed with the instrument, even though you, as the proud owner, know intimately the shortcomings of your workmanship. But you should know from experience how to improve on this first model. Never be depressed that the violin falls short of the masterpieces of the seventeenth- and eighteenth-century professional makers, whose work should be an inspiration and not an inhibition. Do not be ashamed of hurried workmanship and perhaps even some mistakes. Use the experience to improve techniques and to build confidence, never forgetting that there is always scope for improvement in such things. Always progress, leaving the mistakes behind, but not forgetting them. And years later, when people come to you with their own efforts, and you can see faults and shortcomings, remember how difficult and how personally involving the business of violin making is. Help them and be generous in your praise and encouragement.

Viola.   The back and sides are made from cherrywood and the belly is spruce.

Cello.   The back and sides are made from cherrywood and the belly is spruce.

Part III:

The Cello

'CELLO

© 1988

No 3

½

½

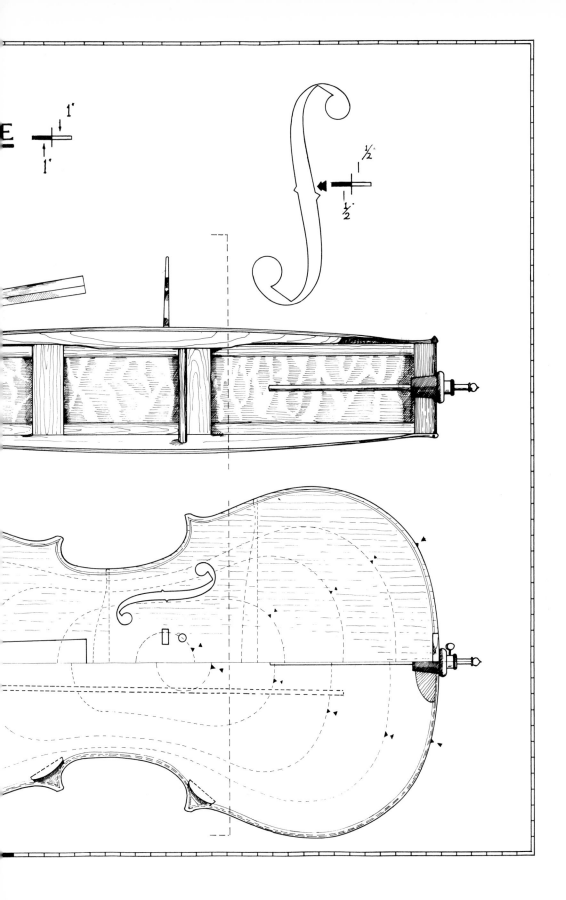

Cello. Cherrywood back and sides, pine belly.

Cello – Construction Sequence

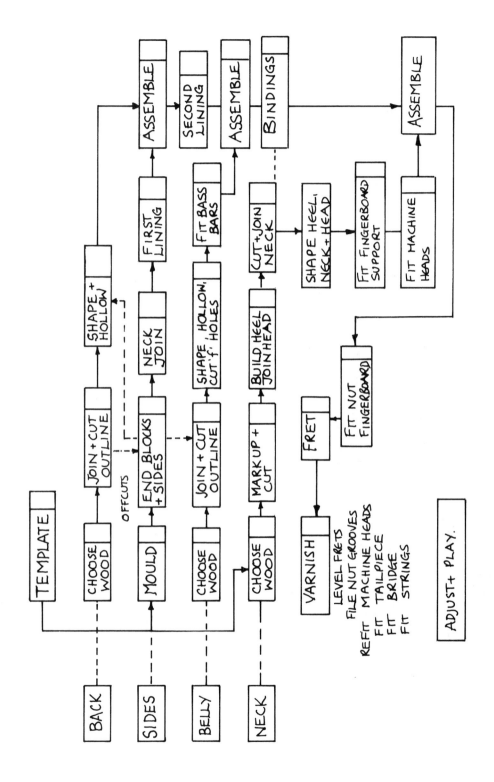

The Cello

The same methods for making a violin and a viola described in the previous pages are used for making a cello. Because of its greater size, the following section will help you surmount the practical problems of working on a larger scale.

Wood

Any wood suitable for making violins is also suitable for cellos. However, it is much more difficult to obtain the large pieces of attractive sycamore for the back and sides at a reasonable price. Because of the size of the instrument, the back and sides have to be interesting and beautiful. If figured sycamore is not available, something equally eyecatching should be chosen instead, with an interesting grain pattern.

Often the most startling grain effects are obtained on slab-sawn woods cut through forks or burrs in the tree trunk. The choice is a wide one – most woods with an interesting, swirling, strongly defined grain should be considered. You could choose alder, poplar, ash, willow, birch, cherry, pear, apple or walnut. Any of these would be satisfactory and all of them, if properly handled, produce a good tone.

Avoid boards with cracks and intergrown knots (these are knots with a black ring round their perimeter). Try to select a piece that is basically sound, but displays a unique appearance. Sometimes woodyards neglect some woodpiles; the wood remains wet for too long and black marks appear on the surface of the wood. These watermarks can be removed with oxalic acid, dissolved in water, but for a cello leave them as they can add interest to its appearance.

Such wood should be cheap, as it is the kind of timber that a sawyer and a cabinet maker is likely to reject. However, one drawback is that slab-sawn wood (particularly that which has confused grain) is likely to warp and twist more than quarter-sawn wood. This tendency will be apparent from the moment the wide wedges are cut, when the sides are likely to spring out of line. Areas of varying densities shrink differently and will continue to move as humidity changes, so that the back and sides will be more undulated after finishing than might be desirable.

The way to minimize this unpredictability is to work the back to shape and bring it to within ¼ in of its final thickness, then leave it in a warm room to dry. After a week or two it will have stabilized. Shave the outer surface and carve the inside to its finished thickness. The same treatment will be required at the sides, which should be selected in such a way that the grain at the corners should be as straight and clean as possible to facilitate bending.

Thicknesses

The plans give the suitable thicknesses for the back and the belly. Remember that the cello is a particularly vulnerable, fragile and cumbersome instrument, and easily damaged. The belly at the edges is particularly vulnerable, and should not be too thin. The thickness of the back can be gauged by springing the back as described on page 69 and tapping it for resonance. Thinner-backed cellos often sound better than heavier models.

The sides

Cutting the sides

Owing to their width it is quite often impossible to make the sides from the wedges cut from the back, and a separate block of similar wood may be required. When you have smoothed the outer face you can then saw this by hand.

If you have a well-equipped toolshop you can

easily make a cut of the required size, but for those who have smaller machines, the best technique for accurately cutting thick stock is to square the piece, run it over the circular saw with the fence set to the correct width of cut, invert it to make a second cut, and then slice between the sawcuts to release the sides with a bandsaw or a handsaw.

Setting up the mould

Because the sides of the cello are wide, the corner and end blocks must be set up accurately to ensure that they are at right angles to the face of the mould. The procedure is described on page 45. Once the mould is set up and the blocks carved to shape, it is important that the sides be fitted square to the mould, and parallel with each other; otherwise it might be very difficult to remove the mould from inside the sides without causing them damage.

Bending the sides

The curves at the sides of the cello have a larger radius and are probably easier to bend than the sides of the violin. Because of this, it is necessary to keep the wood moving slowly over the hot bending iron and to keep the pressure quite even at all times. Prevent the sides sticking to the mould by slipping strips of newspaper between the sides and the mould. After glueing and levelling the edges, remove the glue blocks and press the mould down-

wards a little. When the sides are ready to be released from the mould, run a knife between the mould and the sides and then pare away the corner blocks, removing the dovetail from each one as illustrated. By slipping the mould one inch sideways, the blocks release themselves and the mould can be taken out.

Assembly

Because of the greater width, the violin clamps will be unsuitable for clamping the back and belly to the sides. Special clamps for this can be made, each clamp utilizing a length of threaded steel rod. The alternative clamps illustrated are easy and cheap, and almost as satisfactory. It is very important that these clamps are reliable and handy. If one of the designs illustrated below is used, make at least 18 – if possible 36 – so that the back or belly can be glued in one operation. In order to make the wooden clamps function efficiently, rub candle wax on their shafts.

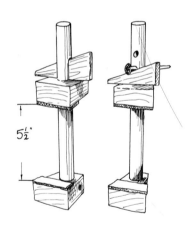

REMOVE DOVETAILS, INVERT MOULD AND
TAP IT DOWNWARDS TO RELEASE SIDES.

Purfling

It is always interesting to experiment, and with a cello one thing that can be introduced with pleasing results is wider purfling. This is easy to make, cut and fit and, particularly if the instrument is rather plain, it will enhance its appearance.

Use sycamore for the core strip of the home-made purfling. Square the edge of a straight-grained offcut, and saw off a strip up to ⅛ in wide for the central core. Smooth both sides with a block plane. A heavy black line each side of the central core would be unsightly. Instead, glue a strip of black, good quality, mounting paper to each side of the core piece, using white woodworkers' PVA glue. Roll the black paper tight against the sides of the core strip. When the glue has dried, trim the bottom edge of the sandwich and cut a strip of purfling with a pointed scalpel, or a thin-bladed steel kitchen knife with small tooth serrations filed into its tip, guiding the tool against a steel straightedge. Cut from both faces towards the centre of the core. In order for the purfling to bend easily, the strip should be at least as deep as it is wide. Pre-form the purfling with the bending iron and take particular care over the corners, where mistakes on this scale are likely to be obvious. Because the paper at the sides of the purfling is easily damaged, make certain before fitting that the purfling slides easily into the groove. Glue it in the normal way, rubbing the back of the

purfling with the handle of a gouge to burr and widen the insert once it is pressed into the groove.

The neck, pegbox and scroll

It is often difficult to find wood that is sufficiently large and straight for the neck, heel, scroll and pegbox to be cut in one piece. It is usually necessary, and more economical, to make them from three or more pieces, assembling them after the preliminary shaping is completed.

Making the heel

The heel is made from a number of well-seasoned offcuts of sycamore glued together. Although it is not necessary, it is more satisfactory to glue them one at a time. Assemble the parts before glueing. When every part of the heel is in position run a centreline from the neck to the tip of the heel. Check each join to ensure that it is satisfactory. Lay out the parts and number them. Dismantle the heel, lightly abrade the glueing surfaces with the teeth of a sharp hacksaw blade and heat the glue.

Add a little flake white powder to the hot glue, to help disguise the glueline, and add a drop of water so that it is easy to apply. Fit one piece at a time, quickly brushing on the glue. Twist and press the glued pieces together. Screw a C-clamp to hold them and protect the surfaces of the blocks and neck with wooden pads. Screw the clamp as tight as possible, and

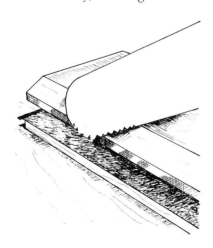

leave the glue to harden. Fit the next piece once the glue has hardened. Never place the neck in bright sunshine or leave it close to a heat source, as the stresses caused by the different contractions of the stacked pieces will cause it to shrink, warp and crack. Smooth the sides and cut out the profile of the heel. Insert a ³⁄₁₆ in thick hardwood reinforcement into its leading face before carving.

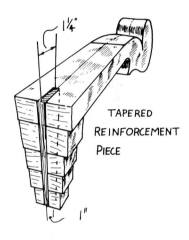

TAPERED
REINFORCEMENT
PIECE

Joining the pegbox and the scroll to the neck

The joint between the pegbox and the neck has to be very strong. As can be seen, the pegbox is wider than the neck, and for maximum strength the scarf must extend to the cheeks of the pegbox as illustrated, giving the greatest glued surface area. The joint is usually made before the pegbox is hollowed, and before the neck is cut to shape. The procedure for making this joint is as follows.

Mark the nut and centreline reference lines on the neck and pegbox. Trim the tip of the neck beyond the nut reference line at the angle shown. Plane the surfaces smooth and check that they are parallel. Square the cut at the underside of the neck to simplify fitting.

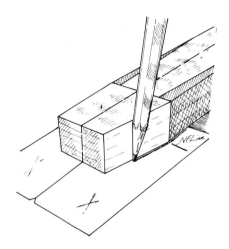

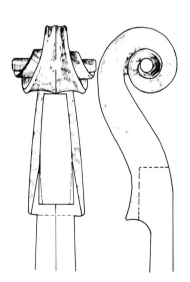

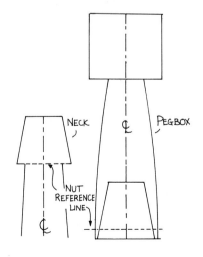

Trace and cut a template of the end of the neck and mark on it the centreline reference. Place this on the pegbox, and position it at the nut reference mark on the centreline of the

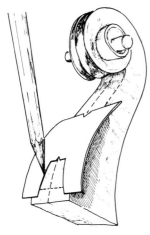

Continue until the joint fits perfectly, checking constantly that the centrelines and the angle of the neck relative to the pegbox remain true.

Once they fit, clamp them together and check their alignment. The only place where the joint is likely to show is at the chin and at the narrow facing edges at the top of the pegbox. This is a highly stressed joint so continue trimming and fitting it until it is satisfactory. No reinforcements, pegs or dowels will supplement the strength of a well glued joint.

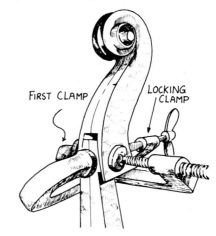

FIRST CLAMP   LOCKING CLAMP

pegbox. Mark round the template, remove it and cut into the lines with a sharp knife. Mark down the cheeks of the pegbox. Strike off the depth of the neck at the joint with a marking gauge.

Saw down the scarf joints, cutting beyond the end marks, but without cutting into the opposite cheeks of the pegbox. Support the underside of the pegbox and chisel away waste between the sawcuts. Keep the chisel at right-angles to the grain. Use a mallet to chop out the waste, working from the edge inwards. Work back to the end of the joint, and perhaps a little further, and smooth down the sides and the bottom of the joint with a bevel-edged chisel and then a file. Rub white chalk onto the neck and insert it into the pegbox. Remove with a chisel the high spots revealed by the chalk residues left on the cheeks and base of the joint.

Size both faces and wipe away the surplus glue. Apply thicker glue and slide the neck quickly into position. Clamp the cheeks. With the heel of the neck resting on the bench, give a

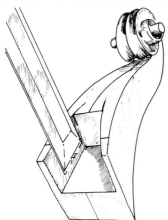

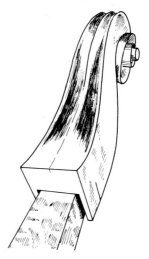

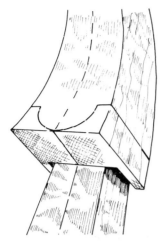

Reaming the hole for the spike

The homemade reamer illustrated and described on page 20 is used to ream the spike hole in the bottom of the cello. The initial hole will have been bored while the sides were still in their mould. Regularly check the angle and depth of the hole by inserting the spike and checking its alignment. A string line dropped from the pegbox over the fingerboard to the tip of the spike will help to establish its alignment.

Fitting up

The drawings for the cello include a template for the curve of the bridge and the string spaces for the bridge and nut. Heights between the string and fingerboard are also included. Pare away all unnecessary wood from the bridge, both at the feet and at the sides and top, and chamfer the sides as illustrated.

few taps on the top of the scroll, then fit the second clamp between the face of the neck and the back of the scroll. Leave the glue to harden. Trim to shape when the glue is dried in the order illustrated.

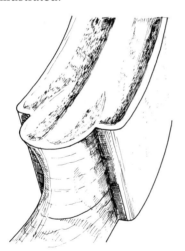

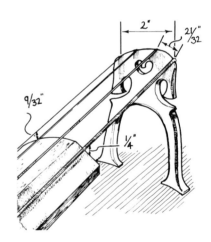

Part IV:

The Mandolin and Mandola

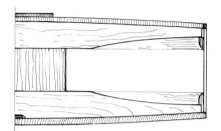

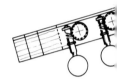

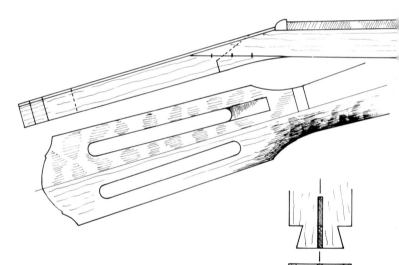

No. 4

MANDOLIN

© 1988

SCALE

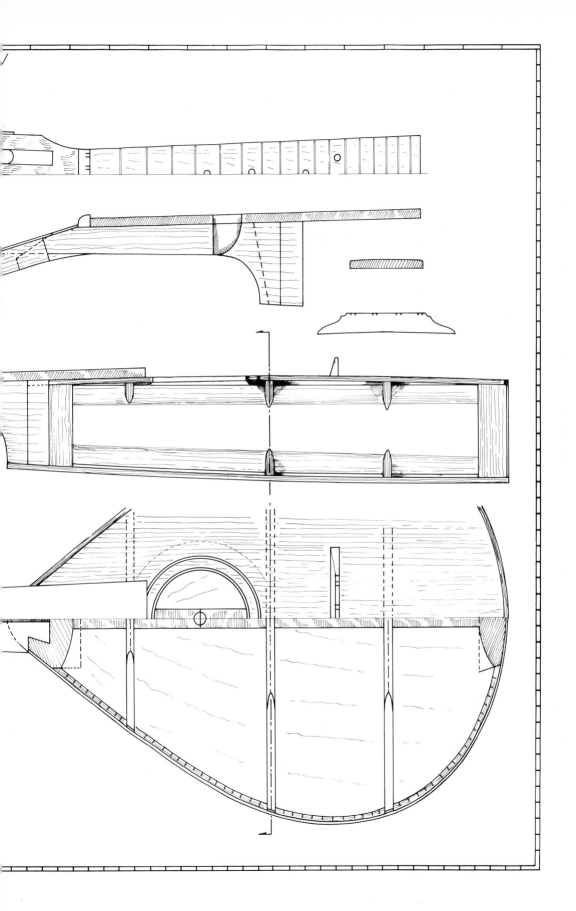

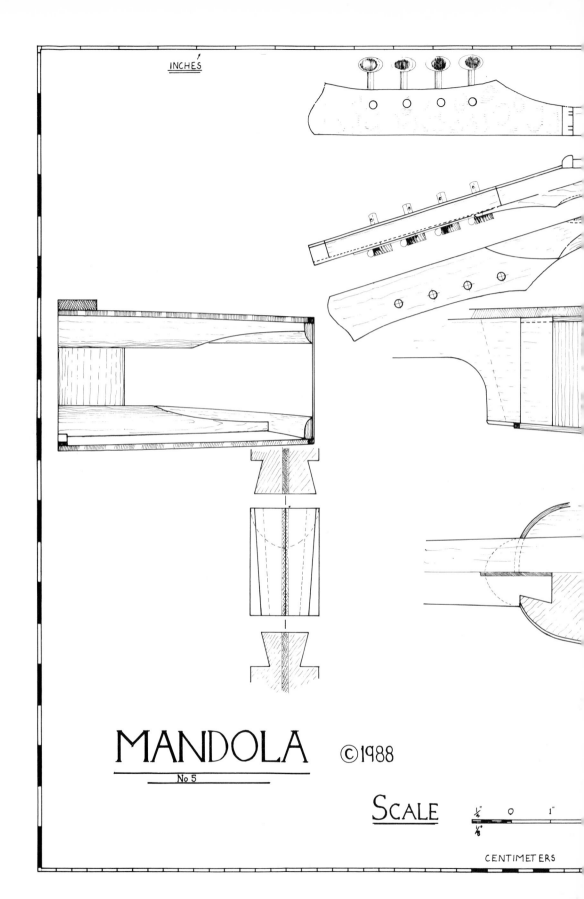

INCHES

MANDOLA ©1988
No 5

SCALE
¼" 0 1"
⅛"

CENTIMETERS

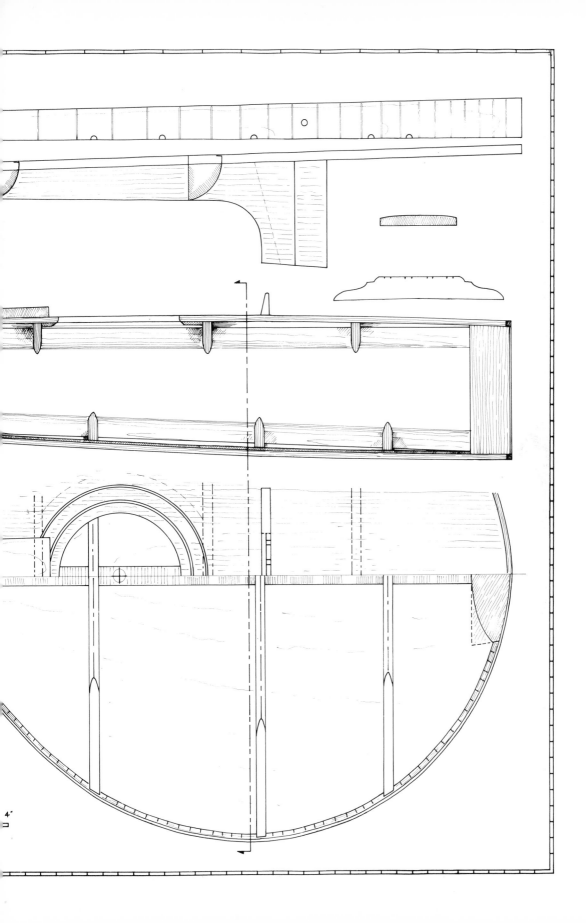

4"

Mandolin. Birch back and sides, pine belly,
mahogany neck.

Mandola. Sycamore back and sides, spruce belly, mahogany neck.

Mandolin & Mandola – Construction Sequence

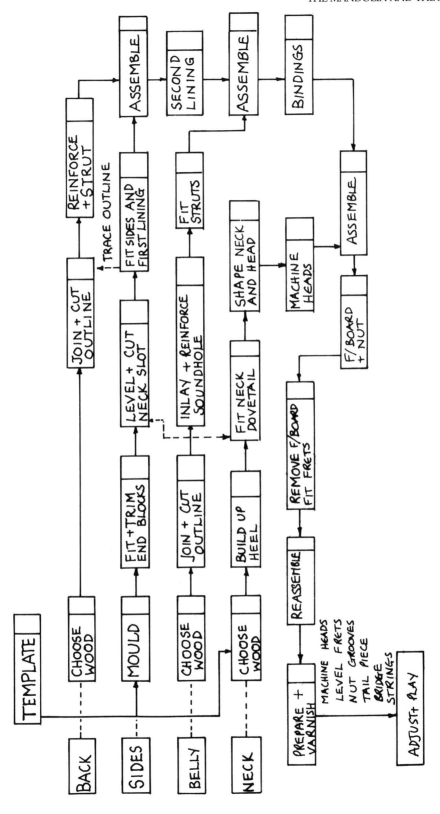

The Mandolin and Mandola

These are fretted instruments, tuned in fifths. The mandolin, which is the smaller of the two, is tuned to the same pitch as the violin. The mandola is tuned to *G, D, A, E,* but an octave lower than the violin, and has a greater string length. Each instrument has eight steel strings, which are tuned in pairs.

The drawing opposite clearly shows the heaviness of the neck/body join, and the strutting which is used to reinforce and tension the back and belly. The back and belly are made from flat boards, slightly swelled by the addition of curved struts glued beneath them. The sides are made from two pieces.

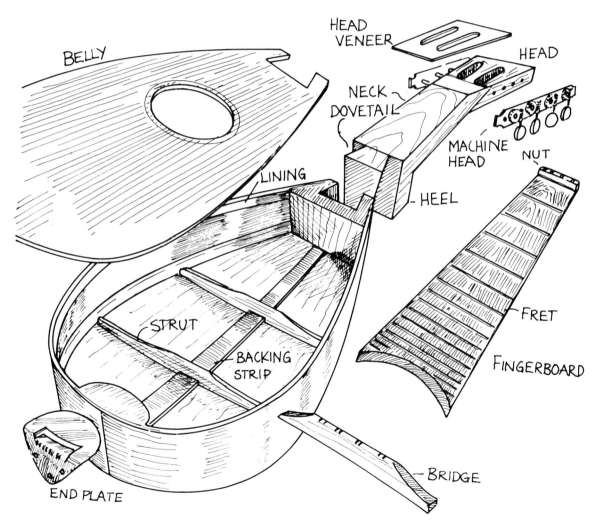

151

Because of the number of strings, the neck/body joint is under much greater stress than that of the violin. This accounts for the heavier construction of this joint in both these instruments. With no corners to catch, purfling is unnecessary. However, because these suffer fairly rough usuage, it is worthwhile fitting bindings at the very edges to protect the edges of the back and belly from snagging. These are not shown in the construction drawing.

The strings are tensioned by machine screws installed in the underside of the head, or are fitted at the sides. Machine heads can be purchased from the instrument makers' suppliers listed in the Appendix.

Construction

The diagrams below outline the construction of the mandolin and mandola. Although the scale of the instruments varies, changes are catered for in the plans available from the suppliers listed at the back of the book. The only additional skill required to those that have already been described in detail earlier in the book, and which might cause difficulty, is the technique for cutting the powerful dovetail joint at the heel of the neck. This operation is performed early in the construction in order to ensure that the major requirement of a strong neck/body join at the correct angle is fulfilled.

Wood and adhesive

The back, sides and often the neck are made from matching hardwood. The belly is made from softwood. Almost any woods can be used. The choice for the back and sides should depend upon the visual appeal of the wood. Honduras mahogany is a traditional wood for these instruments – it combines beauty with a fairly light weight, which is particularly advantageous for the neck. Walnut and sycamore are also very suitable. Quarter-sawn close-grained silver spruce, or Douglas fir are ideal for the belly. End blocks, bars and linings should be made from willow or spruce, to be as light as possible.

Almost any woodworking glue which will withstand the heavy use these instruments can

be expected to endure is suitable. The hot hide glue favoured by violin makers is satisfactory, except that it is not waterproof. Instructions describing its use are on page 27. Urea-formaldehyde glues are satisfactory, being both extremely strong and waterproof. Care, however, should be taken using the two-part urea-formaldehyde and resorcinol resin glues, as these will stain some hardwoods, including Honduras mahogany. PVA woodworkers' glue is convenient and simple to use and its flexibility is an advantage when the instrument resonates.

Rosewood can be a troublesome wood to glue. It is usually best if the glueing faces of the rosewood are washed in petrol and allowed to dry before glueing, otherwise its slight oiliness can impair the glue bond.

The sides

Making the mould
Once the cardboard template of the overall body shape is obtained, draw in on one side of the template the thicknesses of the sides of the instrument and cut round that line with a scalpel on one half of the template.

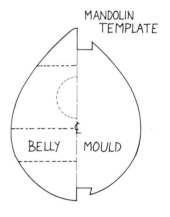

Mark in the positions for the two end blocks and then draw in the dovetailed shape that the bottom block will need in order to wedge in place while the sides are bent and fitted. The block at the bottom of the instrument is an anchorage point for the strings and provides the glueing surfaces for the sides, back and belly. The block at the neck should be heavier to accommodate the substantial dovetail cut into it. The twisting forces imposed by the neck have to be dissipated onto the belly, sides and back, without causing local distortions to the belly.

Once the size and slots for the blocks and the inner side line for the mould have been drawn in on one side of the mould, cut around the edge of the cardboard template to its centreline. Mark the mould outline on a piece of suitable plywood or blockboard and cut out the outline for the mould.

If the instrument has a depth of 2 in or more, a second mould should be made, identical to the first, and fitted to the first with spacers bolted or screwed to the inside faces of the mould so that they can be dismantled after the sides and the first linings have been fitted. All bolt holes fastening the spacers, the outlines and the joints cut into the mould should be cut and drilled together to prevent distorting the mould before the blocks and the sides are fitted.

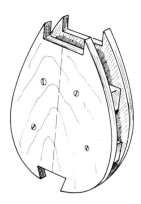

Once the mould is made, fit the end blocks into the slots with a spacer set beneath the mould on the underside to provide room for the linings at that side. Slip the blocks into place, and glue them there with a small glue block on each side of the mould. Leave the glue to harden.

Trimming the blocks

Take the mould with its two end blocks firmly held in place by the small glue blocks. Use a straightedge and set square or a long piece of straightedged cardboard to mark onto the end blocks the centrelines on each side of the mould. Mark one side 'Belly' and the other 'Back'.

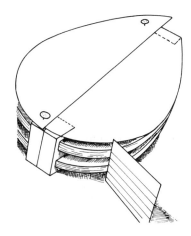

With the belly uppermost, pin the cardboard template over the mould, check its accurate alignment with a filing card or set square, and transfer the curves of the sides onto the end grain of the blocks. Trim the bottom end block to the line. Redraw the centreline on the end block. Invert the mould and, using the accurate shape of the block as a reference point, set the template over the back and repeat on the other side. Trim the neck block to shape, finishing with a file to ensure that its surfaces are parallel with the sides of the mould.

Then, trim the end grain of the bottom block. This should be slightly bevelled to allow for the slight swelling of the back and belly. Trim this line with a block plane, set very fine, and smooth it with a file. Re-establish centrelines before trimming the neck block.

The sides of the mandolin taper towards the neck. Shorten the neck block to fit the taper drawn on the plans. Saw about ¼ in from the back of the block. Angle the cut so the taper and the slight swelling of the back are accommodated. The top face of the neck block should be bevelled to fit against the slight curve of the

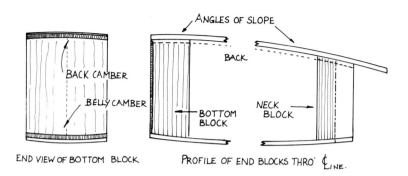

END VIEW OF BOTTOM BLOCK   PROFILE OF END BLOCKS THRO' ₵ LINE.

belly. Do not worry about slight damage to the inner edges of the blocks. These will be trimmed and faired after the sides are fitted, and it is likely that any damage will be removed then.

Cutting and fitting the neck

Select a piece of suitable wood for the neck. If the sides and the back are made from Honduras mahogany, then the neck should also be made from the same timber. Test the piece thoroughly for weaknesses and cracks. Avoid any pieces which display a black line across the grain – this is a weakness line. Suspend the piece between the thumb and first finger and tap it to check resonance. A good board will resonate clearly.

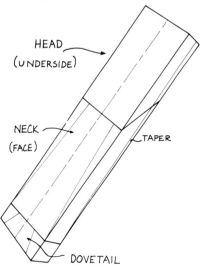

The length of the neck can be taken from the drawings. Remember to add the depth of the dovetail and an additional 8 in for the head. Plane a taper on the underside of the neck/head piece, and then build up the heel in the manner described on page 137 and add a reinforcing piece down its centreline.

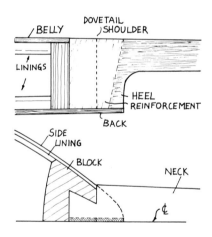

The plans and drawings of the joint illustrated opposite show the major dimensions and reference marks that you use. The neck can be fitted once the end blocks are shaped and the neck and heel cut.

Mark the centreline down the neck and heel. Establish the width of the neck where it meets the end block, not forgetting to add the thickness of the sides at the end blocks, which are concealed by the heel. Mark off on the neck block the joint line and cut this away. Plane it flat, and re-establish centrelines. Mark in the dovetail, with the sides angled to approximately 70 degrees. Note that the dovetail tapers as it passes into the neck block. Approximate a taper to suit the size and depth of the heel and mark this on the back of the neck block. Use a cutting gauge to mark in the depth of the dovetail.

Take a ½ in bevel-edged chisel and lightly pare away the waste from inside the lines of the joint. Notice the bias of the grain and always work so that the chisel lifts out of the joint. Cut precisely to the line, making the finishing cuts by starting the chisel in the gauge line. Level the joint with a flat half-round file if necessary.

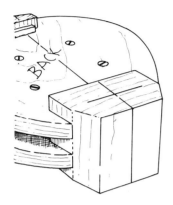

Cutting the dovetail slot

Hold the mould in the vice with the neck block uppermost. Use a backsaw to cut down the sides of the dovetail. Make an additional cut down the middle of the joint if the dovetail is more than ¾ in wide at the belly. Stop the sawcuts at the gauge mark.

Cutting the dovetail

Provided that the marks on the heel are adequate and accurate, this is a fairly straight-forward operation. First, plane the joining face of the heel to give the fingerboard its tilt. The correct angle can be taken from the drawings, but it can also be marked directly by setting the belly face down on a pair of battens and leaning the neck against the body of the instrument, packing pieces beneath the ends to give it its correct angle. Once the neck and the body are

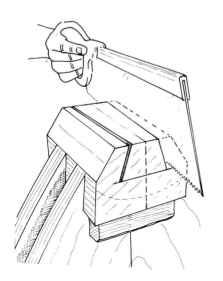

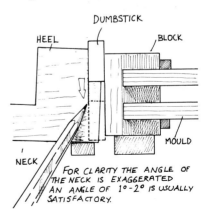

DUMBSTICK

HEEL

BLOCK

MOULD

NECK

FOR CLARITY THE ANGLE OF THE NECK IS EXAGGERATED AN ANGLE OF 1°-2° IS USUALLY SATISFACTORY.

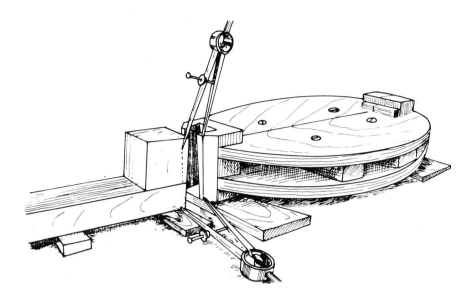

set up, the angle for the heel can be drawn in, using a dumb stick or a pair of compasses.

Square off and cut the new line. Smooth the face of the heel before redrawing the centre-line.

Gauge in the shoulder line of the dovetail at the top face of the neck and bottom of the heel. Then set the gauge to the thickness of the belly, plus 1/16 in for adjustment, and gauge a height line across the face of the heel. The dovetail is inserted into the neck block to this line. This allows for the thickness of the belly, which is fitted later.

Measure down from the height line the depth of the neck block. Square this off and mark in the widths of the dovetail at these top and bottom marks, referring to the dovetail slot cut in the neck block and using dividers to transfer the dimensions. Using a template or angle bevel, mark in the dovetail angles, then use the angle bevel again to mark in the shoulders of the dovetail, with the same setting used for marking in the jointing face of the heel.

Cut the dovetail sides, stopping each cut when the saw reaches the shoulder lines.

Place the neck in the vice, relieve the waste side of the shoulder lines with a chisel, then saw off the shoulders to relieve the waste.

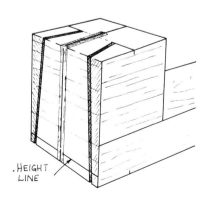

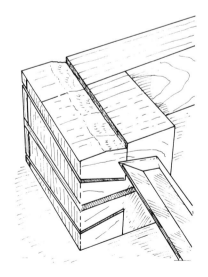

Fit the dovetail. It should slide into and through the neck block, stopping at the height line, leaving a little protruding through the bottom of the neck block for trimming. If the dovetail is too wide, file or chisel it until it fits. If there is a slight gap between the shoulders and the neck block, check first that the shoulders are square, not forced apart by small shavings. If the shoulders are square and clean, it may be necessary to remove a shaving from the face of the dovetail and then refit the neck. Trim the joint until it slides into the recess, with the mark flush with the end block. Even slight sloppiness in this joint is unacceptable, but it is easy to rectify bad workmanship by inserting a thin slither of veneer on each side, against the sides of the dovetail. This reinforces the edges of the block and also the weak short grain of the dovetail when it is glued in place.

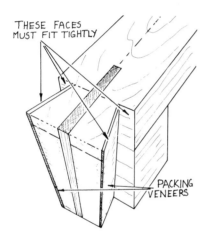

THESE FACES MUST FIT TIGHTLY

PACKING VENEERS

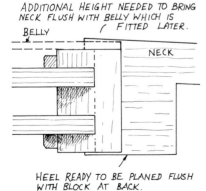

ADDITIONAL HEIGHT NEEDED TO BRING NECK FLUSH WITH BELLY WHICH IS FITTED LATER.

BELLY

NECK

HEEL READY TO BE PLANED FLUSH WITH BLOCK AT BACK.

Trim the dovetail until its heel is slightly proud of the block at the back, and the height line on the face of the neck is level with the top of the neck block.

Use a string line to check that the neck is true with the centreline of the mould. Slight misalignments are acceptable, as the neck has yet to be tapered and, if absolutely necessary, the centreline of the bottom block can be altered slightly. Press the neck into place, and plane the heel flush with the back of the neck block.

Fitting the sides

Remove the neck. The sides are cut, bent and fitted in exactly the same way that the cello and violin sides are fitted. The additional width of the two-piece mould makes the fitting and accurate alignment of the sides a little easier than on the violin. Fit the butt join at the bottom block before springing the sides around the mould. Glue them to the top block. Bring the sides past the glueing face of the neck joint. Do not cut them to length until after the glue has set.

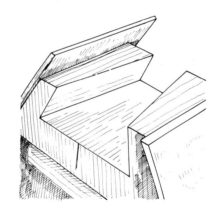

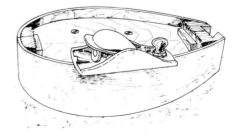

Cut the sides to lie just proud of the glueing face of the neck join. Plane them flush with the end block. Use the cardboard straightedge to mark in the width and taper of the sides. Cut them with a chisel and clean up the line with a block plane. Do not release the sides from the mould until the back and belly have been made.

The back

The back is made from one or more pieces of hardwood, approximately 1/8 in thick. Thickness the pieces before the joints are shot, and before the parts are assembled. If the back is made from several pieces, try to match the woods so that the grains repeat their patterns over the back of the instrument. Smooth each piece on both sides, using a block plane sharpened to a steep cutting angle to prevent the grain tearing out. Wax the sole of the plane to ease its movement over the wood.

Shooting the joints

Two methods for shooting the joint in the back are described. If a long soled plane is available, the former will be the quickest and simplest method. Otherwise, a combination of the two may be necessary.

Pair the pieces for the back, and mark their face sides. Stack them, face sides together, and shoot the joint in one operation, resting the pieces on a shooting board. When they are separated and laid together, any slight bevel caused by the plane iron will be cancelled by the same, but opposite bevel on the second piece, so that the pieces should lie flush and true.

An alternative method, necessary when a long soled plane is not available, is to shoot each join separately. Align each joint line separately to the edge of the shooting board, and with the blade of the block plane adjusted to give a vertical and fine cut, plane down the edge of the board. Once the plane has removed

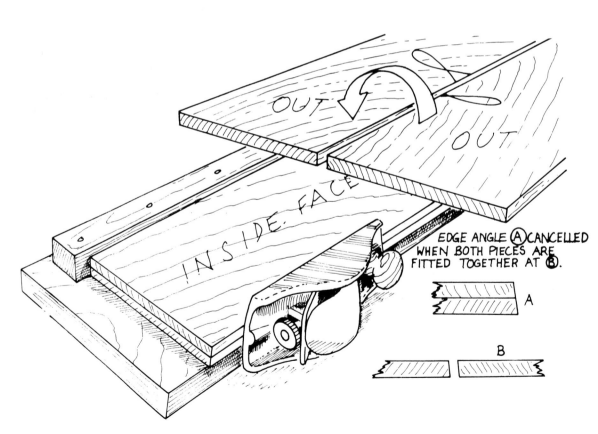

EDGE ANGLE (A) CANCELLED WHEN BOTH PIECES ARE FITTED TOGETHER AT (B).

the splintered edge and left a clean cut, replace the board with its pair and shoot the second edge. Place both boards on a flat surface, and slide the edges together. If only a short soled plane is used, it is unlikely that the longitudinal line will be true. Chalk one edge and rub the second against it, easing away the chalk traces left by the board. This is a very simple operation, provided that the plane is set to its finest cut and the strip is always set in the shooting board with the same face uppermost each time.

Even without pressure, the joints should be satisfactory, and if there are black lines which show a cavity between the strips, the faulty joints should be reshot until they fit properly. Once they fit, practise a dry run through the assembly before glueing and clamping them together. Remember to place strips of newspaper between supporting battens and wedges before applying glue to the joining faces.

Use the string and wedges technique illustrated below to hold the pieces while

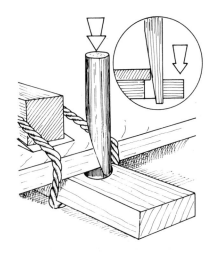

Once the glue has set, remove the back from the clamps and scrape away the glue residue with a cabinet scraper. Scrape the inside face, then invert the board and clean up the outer surface. Finish smoothing with 180 and then 220 grit paper.

Fitting the struts

First cut, fit and glue a cross-grained backing strip over the joint, stopping the strip just short of the end blocks. It will help the strip to lie flat as the glue dries if the glue is applied to both faces of the strip. Once the glue is dry, chamfer

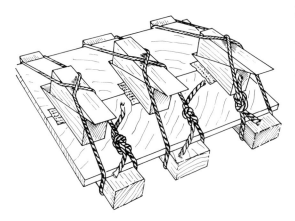

glueing. Some additional sideways force can be applied by inserting wedge-cut dowels into the backing battens as illustrated.

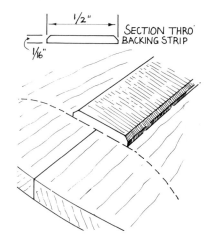

or bevel the edges to fair it into the board. Remove the backing strip when you have planed and sanded the joint before the struts are fitted.

Trace onto the back the outline for the mandolin. Cut around this line, leaving about ⅛ in waste all round. Cut three bars from straight-grained spruce, cut on the quarter, and square them to the sizes illustrated in the plans. They will be fitted across the inside of the back of the instrument to stiffen and pull it into a gentle curve. Position the struts as shown in the plans, measuring from the base of the instrument, not the neck. Cut them to length, leaving about one inch proud at each end, then take them all together, mark off their centrelines, place them in the vice and, with the shoulder plane and file, shave a gentle curve over their upper faces. The maximum height at the middle of the bars should be about ⅛ in.

Glue these to the back, making sure that the back is in full contact with the face of the bars by bending a light flexible strip of pine over the outside before fitting the C- or spring clamps at the edges. The soundbar clamp illustrated will also be effective in ensuring that there is satisfactory contact between the glued surfaces. Leave the back to dry. Trim the ends of the struts and pare down the sides and inner edges shortly before fitting the back to the sides.

The belly

Choose some quarter-sawn spruce or Douglas fir for the belly. Select pieces that have a close straight grain, and if necessary join several strips for a regular and even grain pattern over the width of the belly. Smooth and join the pieces as described. Plane and sand the outer face before marking in and cutting the outline for the belly, allowing about ⅛ in waste beyond the cutting line. Mark in the position for the soundhole, and on the underside of the belly the positions for the struts.

Mark in the soundhole and draw a second line approximately one inch further out, which will be the limit for the reinforcement. Use a pair of waste pieces cut from the outline of the belly for the reinforcement, and with the grain parallel to the grain of the belly, mark and cut the outside shapes of the reinforcement. Glue them in place, clamping them with two strong battens to sandwich the reinforcement and the

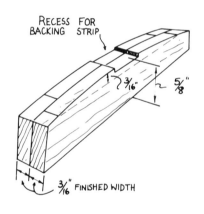

RECESS FOR BACKING STRIP

³⁄₁₆"   ⅝"

³⁄₁₆" FINISHED WIDTH

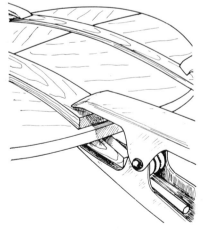

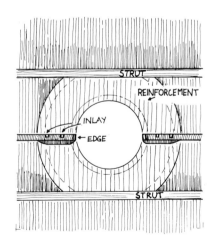

STRUT

REINFORCEMENT

INLAY

← EDGE

STRUT

*Guitar.   Made from mahogany and pine, with
ebony and sycamore inlay.*

Guitar. Made from figured sycamore.

belly together. When the glue is dry, shave down the reinforcement until it is no more than 1/16 in thick. The reinforcement helps anchor the inlay cutter, as well as providing a layer to support the inlay at the edge of the soundhole.

Inlaying and cutting a circular soundhole

A special cutter for incising the line will be required, as illustrated. It is adjusted by moving the block which holds the 1/4 in steel pivot. This locates in a hole bored in the centre of the soundhole. Such a tool can be made from any offcut of hardwood, the blade being fashioned from a scalpel blade or a used jigsaw blade.

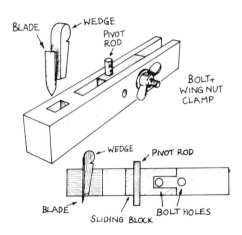

Mark the centrepoint for the soundhole and bore a 1/4 in hole vertically through it.

Before starting to work on the inlay, have a clear idea of the style and complexity of the design desired. It is, after all, only the perimeter of a hole being decorated. Too ornate or complex a pattern might concentrate attention on the unattractive interior of the instrument. Perhaps a few concentric lines of inlay are all that is required, with an additional strip at the inner edge of the soundhole to bind and protect its edge.

Work outwards from the smallest diameter inlay to the greatest. In this way, the fragile sides of the grooves are always protected by the bulk of the belly.

Set the cutter to the dimension for the smallest circle required. With the cutter blade positioned with its sharpening bevel facing outwards, locate the fence over the hole in the belly and incise a circle. Continue cutting until the full depth of the inlay has been reached. This should be about 1/16 in. The depth of the blade can easily be adjusted by sticking a slither or two of veneer with adhesive tape under the arm of the cutter, preventing it from cutting too deeply.

Once the first cut is made, readjust the tool, turn the blade and cut the second line the precise width of the inlay. Remove the waste with a purfling chisel. Bend and insert the inlay as described on pages 92-4, butting the joint at right angles beneath the position of the fingerboard.

Cut the second groove in the same way. If a wider groove is wanted for a marquetry inlay, cut the incisions in the same way, then make and fit a simple router blade into the arm of the inlay cutter to remove the waste to an even depth.

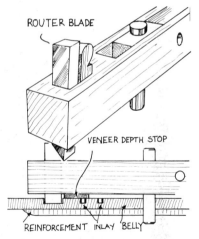

Cut and shape the inlay as illustrated, then insert it, filling gaps between pieces with pigmented glue. Fit the perimeter inlay last. Cut this to the full depth of the table and remove the waste right up to the level of the reinforcement glued beneath the belly. Insert the inlay and leave the glue to harden. Trim down the decoration with the shoulder plane, scrapers and sandpaper. Then refit the cutter with the

161

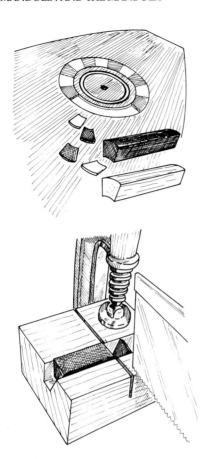

Bevel the reinforcement from the edge of the soundhole so that it is invisible when viewed from the surface of the belly.

Cutting and inlaying an elliptical soundhole

An elliptical soundhole can look very attractive, but because of the difficulty of setting up a mechanical trammel to cut an ellipse it is necessary to cut the soundhole first, and then to use the purfling tool to mark in positions for the inlay strips, using the edge of the hole to bear against. The ellipse is constructed in the following way:

Decide the exact sizes for the major and minor axes of the ellipse. The major axis lies at right angles to the centreline of the belly. Lightly pencil in the major and minor axes. Set a pair of compasses to half the major axis. Position the compass over the end point of the minor axis and strike off the two points where the arc drawn from the end of the minor axis intersects the major axis. These are the two focal points of the ellipse. If a circle of thread is looped over two drawing pins, each fixed at the focal points, and a pencil is hooked into the loop (as illustrated) the line drawn by the pencil pulling against the loop will describe the ellipse of the desired size.

adjustment set to cut away at the end edge of the last piece of inlay. Incise the soundhole on the outer surface of the belly and then invert the belly to release the waste from the underside.

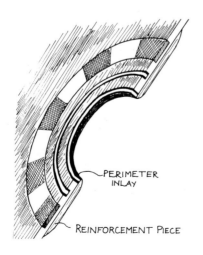

PERIMETER INLAY

REINFORCEMENT PIECE

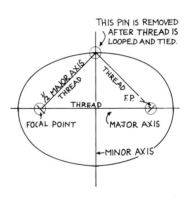

THIS PIN IS REMOVED AFTER THREAD IS LOOPED AND TIED.

½ MAJOR AXIS
THREAD
THREAD
THREAD
F.P.
FOCAL POINT
MAJOR AXIS
MINOR AXIS

Cut around the line with a scalpel then, using a fretsaw, cut to the line and remove the waste from the centre of the soundhole. Trim the inside edge of the soundhole with a penknife and smooth it with a hard leather pad wrapped with 150 grit paper.

Use the purfling tool to make incisions for the inlay, bearing the fence of the tool against the inside of the ellipse. When the decorative inlay has been inserted and glued, cut the incision for the inside edge of the soundhole. Then fit the reinforcement piece beneath the soundhole. This supports the inlay while it is being glued. Glue the inlay into position, holding it in place with pins and adhesive tape. Finally, trim the inlay to its correct height, trim the reinforcement to $1/16$ in thick and fair its outer edge.

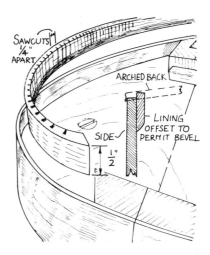

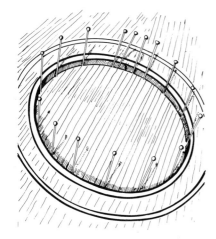

Fitting the struts to the belly

Cut and fit struts onto the belly. These are shaped and curved as described for the back and serve to stiffen and strengthen the belly. Leave about one inch of bar at each edge of the instrument to help to mark the linings when fitting the belly against the sides.

Assembly and finishing

Fitting the linings

Release the glue blocks holding the neck and end block. Slip a thin blade around the edge of the mould to check that the sides are not glued to the mould. Cut and fit the back linings as described on page 58. These are wider and deeper than those of a violin. They are illustrated opposite. To facilitate bending, small sawcuts $3/16$ in apart can be cut around the inside face of the lining. Clamp them at close intervals with spring clothes pegs. Trim the

linings with a block plane, bevelling them upwards from the sides to allow for the slight swelling of the back. Free the mould from the sides and blocks, and remove them before glueing on the back.

Fitting the back

Before the back is fitted, the struts glued to its inside have to be shaped and trimmed to length. First shape the bars to a rounded taper using a bevel-edged chisel and a plane. Mark in from the edges the point where the end tapers start. Trim the bars to the shape illustrated, leaving the ends protruding beyond the edges of the back.

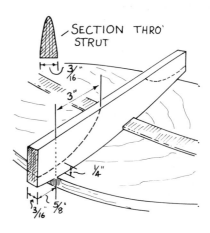

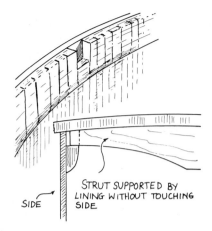

SIDE

STRUT SUPPORTED BY LINING WITHOUT TOUCHING SIDE

Fit the back over the sides. Align the centre-lines and position the back in relation to the end blocks. Pencil onto the linings the location and width of each bar at the point where it crosses the linings. Saw and trim a notch in the linings where the bar meets the sides and then cut the bars a little short so that they do not press against the sides of the instrument. Adjust the bevels at the linings and blocks until the back fits easily into position. Tighten a C-clamp over each block and check its fit.

Glueing the back to the sides

If sufficient numbers of adequately sized violin clamps are available this is a straightforward glueing operation, as described on page 85. If there are not enough clamps, proceed as follows. First loosen the mould and ensure that it can be removed once the back is in place. Position the sides of the instrument belly face downwards on a smooth flat board. Tack finishing nails about 2 in away from the edge of the instrument at regular 2 in intervals.

Bend the heads of the pins away from the body of the instrument. Apply glue to the sides, linings and blocks. Fit the back, then hold it down with long thin rubber bands, stretched across the back and hooked onto the pins around the perimeter of the instrument.

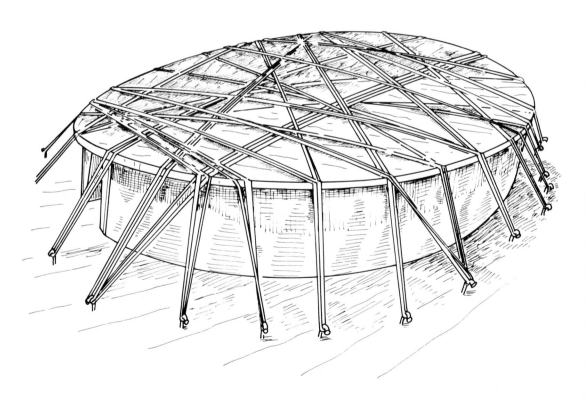

After the glue has hardened, remove the bands and trim the edges of the instrument with a penknife or chisel. Finish with a file. Remove the mould from inside and fit the side linings for the belly. Trim the sound bars and fit and glue on the belly, holding it in the same way as the back, but with the back cushioned onto a soft foam or felt to protect it against bruising. Trim the edges with a knife as described.

Fitting the bindings

The bindings are thin strips inlaid at the edges of the instrument to decorate and provide a hard wearing edge to the softwood of the belly and the hard, often splintery, back. Cut the bindings from some suitable straight-grained hardwood. If a white sycamore binding is used, glue some black mounting paper to one side to contrast with the light tone of the belly.

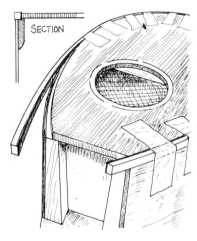

Run the bindings through the thickness trimmer as described on page 94. Each binding should be square section, and slightly oversize to allow for trimming. Set a cutting gauge or purfling gauge to the depth of the binding and mark around the edges of the instrument. Use the same setting to incise the line in the edge of the belly. Remove the waste between the lines with a scalpel. Fit and glue the bindings, and hold them with transparent self-adhesive tape. When the glue has hardened, peel off the tape very carefully, particularly on the soft-wood belly, and smooth down the bindings until they are flush with the side and face of the instrument. If a back binding is required, it is glued and taped in place once the neck is fitted, and joined at the bottom block.

The head and neck

Refer to the plans to calculate the correct length for the neck. The head is spliced to the neck and tilts back at approximately 20 degrees.

Mark in the position for the nut with a knife and set square. Mark a second line $\frac{3}{16}$ in beyond, and parallel to the first, for the position of the nut's upper edge. This is at the break in the angle between the neck and head. Mark this angle on the sides of the neck with an angle bevel, and square around the underside of the neck. Saw to the line and keep the offcut for the head of the instrument.

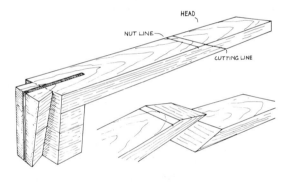

Leave the sawn edge of the neck, but plane up the jointing face of the head and tooth it lightly with a hacksaw blade. Set the head into position and check its fit and angle.

Once the glueing face of the head is smoothed and level, join it to the neck. This smooth splice is difficult to clamp because the pressure of the clamp forces the joint apart and makes tightening and accurate alignment impossible. Various block clamping methods can be used to hold the joint, but these are often less satisfactory than pinning the joint, as described below.

165

Pinning the head joint

Drive two or three small cut nails into the glueing face of the head, and cut them almost flush with the surface of the glue joint.

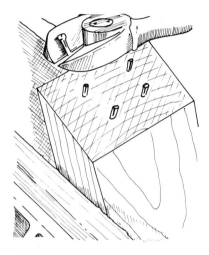

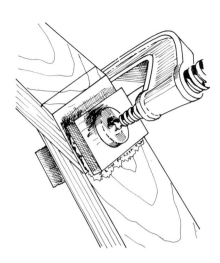

Carefully align the head and neck centrelines and, using hand pressure, squeeze the two faces together. The nails will dent the back of the neck. Deepen these dents with a bradawl to sink the pins. Glue the surfaces and assemble the joint. Apply moderate pressure until the glue has hardened.

the head. Clamp and glue this to the head, pressing the veneer with a block a little larger than the veneer, with a strip of newspaper interposed between the veneer and the block.

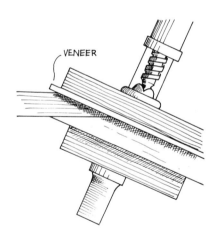

VENEER

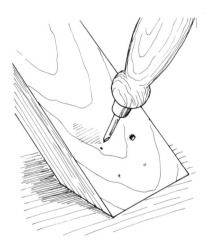

Once the join is dry, smooth the upper face of the head, and trim three thick layers of veneer, or a single ⅛ in offcut from the back to fit over

Shaping the neck and head

Use a template to transfer the shape of the head, cut out the profile of the head with a coping saw, and smooth it with files. The drawing shows the dimensions for the neck taper. The neck should be narrow and comfortable to hold, and the dimensions and section given should be used only as a guide when marking out. Saw the neck taper after the outline for the head has been cut. Fit the neck to a support as described on page 98 and carve the neck and the heel to shape, using flat chisels, planes and files. Finish with a scraper, but leave the edges of the heel where they butt against the sides of the instrument until the neck is glued into the body of the mandolin.

Fitting the machine heads

The holes for the rollers of the machine heads are bored perpendicular to the sides of the instrument head, before the string slots are cut. Choose good quality machine heads, which have a smooth and positive action. A simple design for the brasswork and turns will probably suit the understated beauty of the instrument.

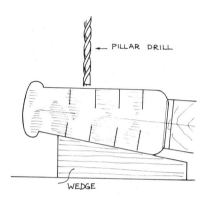

Mark in the positions for the barrel. With a pillar drill and a wedge board, bore each hole, stopping the drill when the length of the barrel has been bored. If a pillar drill is not available make a block from some spare hardwood, and use it as a guide and depth stop as illustrated.

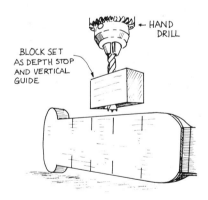

Mark in the positions for the string slots making sure that the ends of the barrels are housed at least ¹⁄₁₆ in in the centre fork of the head. Bore a suitable sized hole at each end of

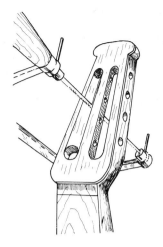

the string slots and remove the waste with a coping saw. Clean up the edges with a flat chisel and bevel the edge closest to the nut to allow the strings to run straight to the barrels. smooth the inner faces of the fork with a sanding block shaped to fit the slot. Fit the machine heads after the instrument has been varnished.

Glueing the neck

Cut away the part of the belly which obscures the slot for the neck dovetail. This is described in some detail on page 112. Press the heel of the dovetail into the body of the instrument, checking that the top surface of the neck is flush with the belly. Carefully trim the face of the neck or the sides and base of the heel until the neck fits.

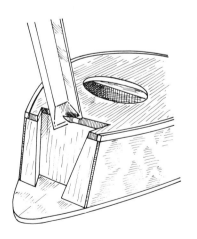

Size the joint and then glue and clamp the neck to the body of the instrument.

When the glue is dry, smooth the edges of the heel and fair it so that the sides appear to lead straight onto the surface of the heel. Fit the back bindings and clean up, and finish smoothing with fine sandpaper, backed against a leather or polyethylene pad.

of the fingerboard. Trim this perfectly, before fitting the fingerboard to the neck and belly.

When the fingerboard rests flat against the neck and belly, mark off the end of the fingerboard, so that it follows either the edge of the soundhole or the line of the outermost strip of inlay at the soundhole. Cut the fingerboard end and then smooth its edge with a file and scrapers.

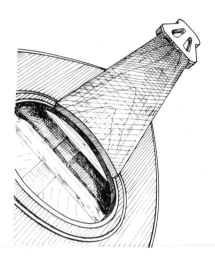

Fitting up

The fingerboard

The fingerboard is made from hardwearing durable wood. Rosewood and ebony are considered best, although beech, sycamore, and some African hardwoods can also be used. True up the undersurface of the board, using an extremely sharp plane honed to a steep sharpening angle. Smooth the outer surface. Square the sides of the fingerboard, mark off, then square across the nut end of the fingerboard. Trim this with a block plane, perhaps finishing with a file if necessary. Then mark the neck taper on the fingerboard, and trim this down with a plane.

Fit the fingerboard against the neck and estimate the angle at which the underside of the fingerboard should be trimmed in order to lie tight against the belly. Mark this with a pencil, and trim the underside with a block plane and scraper, chalking it to a final fit if necessary. If the neck angle is slightly steeper than shown in the plans, fill the gap between the finger-board and belly with a wedge, glued to the underside

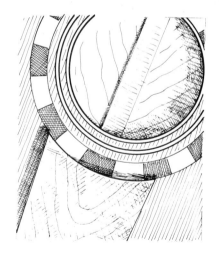

True up the face of the fingerboard with a plane, or with a rough file with its handle removed, bringing it to the slight curve shown in the plans. Finish with wet and dry sandpaper, backed against a felt-covered flat block, to achieve a satin-smooth finish. The frets can now be fitted, or they can be left until after the fingerboard is glued on.

Glue the fingerboard, clamping it in place with spring clamps and a C-clamp through the soundhole to hold down the end of the fingerboard.

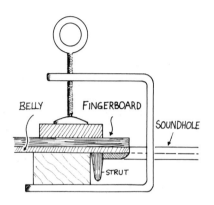

Fitting the frets

You can buy fret wire in a strip and cut it to length. Each fret sits in a sawcut, and its tight fit and the slight roughness of the tang prevent the fret from falling out.

The fret positions are calculated using the Rule of 18 – for any given vibrating string length, the position of the next note up the fingerboard will be 1/18th of that length. Thus as the string length diminishes, so does the distance between the frets.

Mark in the bridge position, and measure the string length from the bridge saddle to the nut. The position of the first fret from the nut is string length divided by 17·835. The position for the second fret is:

$$\frac{\text{string length} - \text{nut to first fret}}{17\cdot835}$$

The frets are fitted at right angles to the centre-line of the fingerboard. Experiment to find this line, holding an angle bevel first on one side of

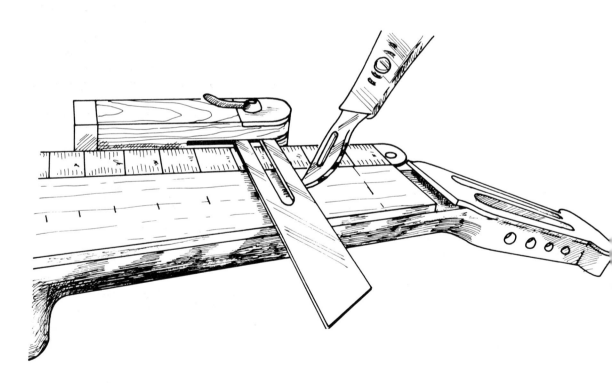

the fingerboard and then the other, pencilling in a fret line and adjusting the angle of the blade until the pencil line is the same from whichever side the bevel is rested. The marks will be more accurate if the bevel is rested against a straight-edge, which in turn rests against the side of the fingerboard.

Use a very sharp pencil. Calculate and then measure in the position of each fret, measuring each fret from the face of the nut.

Make a sample sawcut in a waste piece of hardwood, and press a length of the fret into the cut. The sawcut should be a fraction deeper than the fret tang and sufficiently narrow to grip the sides. If the backsaw has too great a set, lay it on a flat surface, and run a sharpen-ing stone down each side until the set is right.

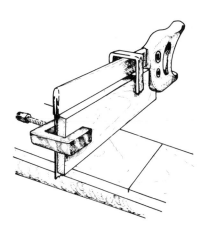

It helps to regulate the depth of the cut. Fix a very thin strip of wood to the side of the saw blade with small metal clamps. After making a few practice saw cuts, and after checking the position of each fret, saw the slots for the frets.

Cut the fret wire approximately to length with a pair of snips or pliers, support the finger-board, and tap the frets into their grooves with a fairly heavy carpenter's hammer. Each fret should bed right down to the fingerboard. When they are all in place file them to length and run a file over the face of the fingerboard to bring the frets to the same height.

If the edges of the frets remain slightly rough, remove them, and file the ends round, then smooth the ends by rubbing them against a sheet of abrasive paper held in the palm of your hand. Before refitting them, it may be necessary to improve their grip in the fingerboard. Take the loose ones, and turn them upside down on a metal block, and make several sharp taps with the back of the hammer against the fret tang. This distorts its edge and gives it a greater hold in the fingerboard. Replace the frets, tapping them into position with a light hammer and a wood block.

Fitting the nut

Once the fingerboard is glued on, the nut can be fitted. This can be made from ebony, ivory, or bone. Buy a suitable bone from the local beef butcher, such as a short length of thigh bone. Scrape it clean and boil it thoroughly. Clean it again, and then soak it in a glass of household bleach to turn it white. Rinse the bone thoroughly and leave it to dry for a week.

Cut a piece from the bone and trim it to shape. Cut the head veneer so that the nut fits exactly between the end of the fingerboard and the veneer, and then mark in, on the upper face of the nut, the level of the head veneer.

Round down to this line with a file and smooth the bone with sandpaper, keeping the edges and corner nearest to the fingerboard square and untouched. Glue the nut into position and file its edges until they coincide exactly with the sides of the fingerboard. Using the dimensions given in the drawing below, file a groove for each string across the nut. Follow,

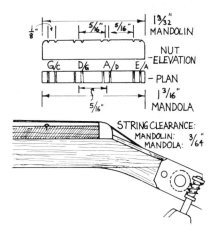

171

using a round rat-tailed file to open up the grooves, so that each string sits snugly into a hole its precise size. Round these grooves at the head so that each string has an easy entry into the nut. Do not round the edge leading onto the fingerboard.

The bridge

The bridge sits on the belly, defining the vibrating string length and transmitting the vibrations of the strings to the belly. Mandolin and mandola bridges are lower and much wider than a violin bridge. The bridge must fit perfectly to the belly. Choose a piece of quarter-sawn hardwood and chalk it down onto the surface of the belly. Once a precise fit is obtained, slightly relieve the underside at the centre of the bridge with a small plane, so that without the string pressure the bridge sits slightly proud of the surface of the belly. Shape the sides and edges of the bridge as illustrated.

Chop out the recess for the string saddle and fit a thin strip of bone for the saddle. Cut notches for the strings as illustrated.

Finish the mandolin using a varnish or catalyst lacquer before screwing the tailpiece into the end block. Fit the machine heads, then string up the instrument.

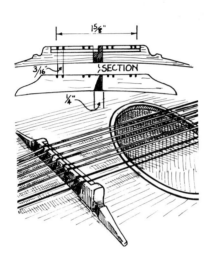

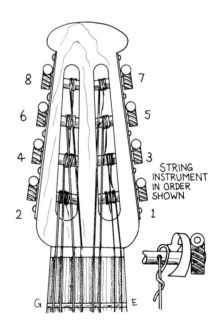

Part V:

The Classical Guitar

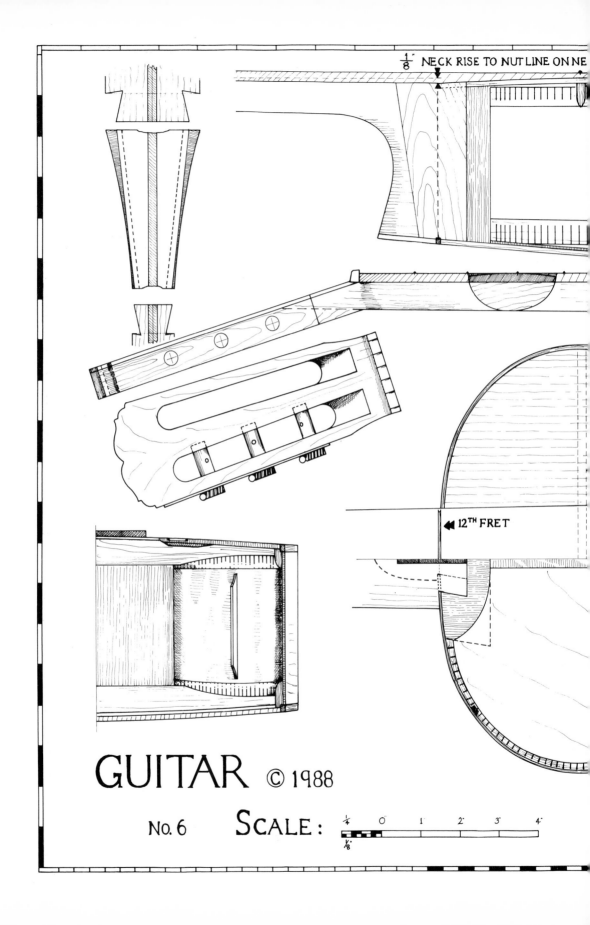

$\frac{1}{8}$" NECK RISE TO NUT LINE ON NE

◀ 12TH FRET

GUITAR © 1988

No. 6   SCALE:

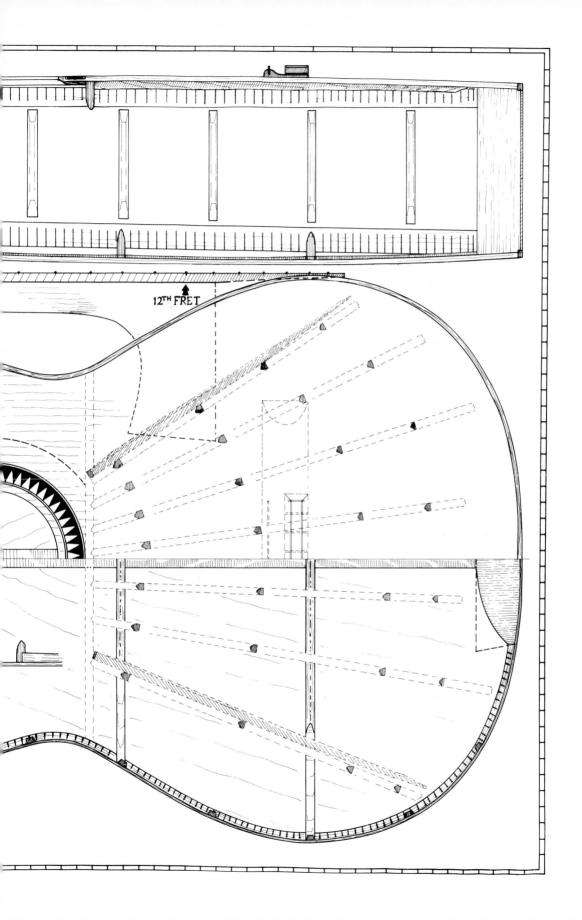

12TH FRET

Classical guitar.

Guitar NO.6 – Construction Sequence

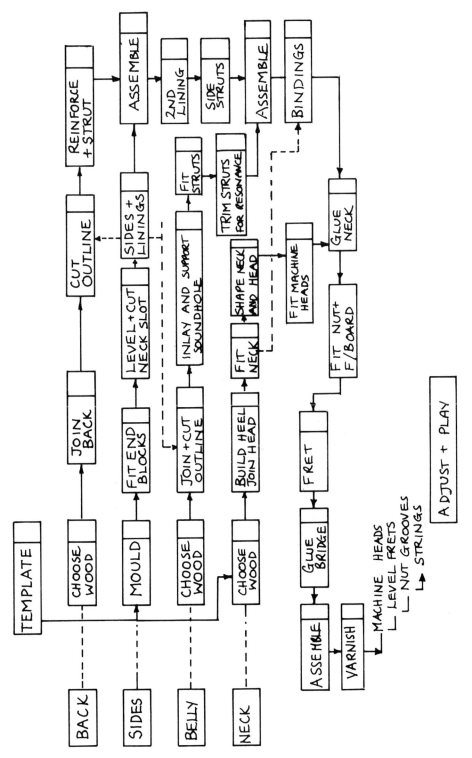

The Classical Guitar

The illustrations and plans below outline the basic components of the classical guitar. The instrument has a waist and continuous sides from the bottom block to the neck block. There are three struts supporting the back of the guitar and a reinforcement strip to cover the joint. Studs are placed on the back to support joins not on the centreline. In addition to its two transverse struts, the belly has fan struts to stiffen and tie the belly together. The strings are terminated at the bridge, which is glued to the belly. The type and pattern of the strutting varies from instrument to instrument, the stiffness and thickness of the belly determining the size and spacing of the struts.

Thick linings are glued to the sides and back, the incisions in their outer faces making them easier to bend. A similar incised lining, or separate glued blocks known as tentellones, help to strengthen the glued join between the belly and the sides. As with the mandolin and the mandola, the neck is joined to the body with a wide and heavy dovetail, tapered towards the heel of the instrument. The neck tilts forwards very slightly, which reduces the string pressure on the belly.

Most of the procedures for making a guitar have already been described in some detail but in a different context elsewhere in the book. The major stages of the construction are

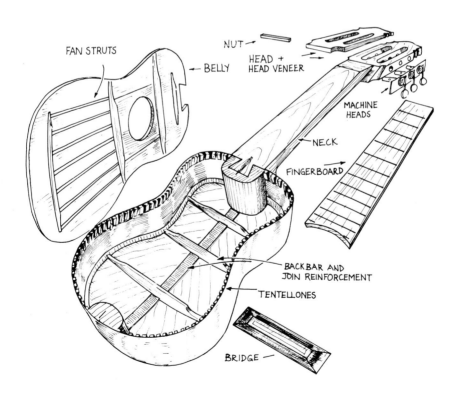

FAN STRUTS

BELLY

NUT

HEAD + HEAD VENEER

MACHINE HEADS

NECK

FINGERBOARD

BACKBAR AND JOIN REINFORCEMENT

TENTELLONES

BRIDGE

outlined below and dealt with in more detail later in this chapter. However, reference will be made to other parts in this book where the descriptions are relevant.

Wood

Any of the woods suggested as suitable for violin, cello, mandolin or mandola making are suitable for guitar making. However, high quality instruments, particularly modern ones, almost invariably have rosewood for the back and sides of the instrument, and often cedar for the neck. For the beginner, the important point is to choose woods that are beautiful and resound well. Rosewood is available in suitable sizes from some of the supply shops mentioned at the back of this book. Walnut or sycamore are also satisfactory.

The belly should be quarter-sawn, resilient, and stiff. Douglas fir, or sitka spruce are acceptable, as are hemlock and Western red cedar. Honduras mahogany is ideal for the neck, being both easily worked, consistent and very beautiful. Struts should be made from stiff pine, quarter-sawn, and blocks from any light-weight straight-grained timber such as sitka spruce.

The sides

The typical shape for a classical guitar is illustrated opposite. A full-sized instrument will have a string length of about 25½ in, with the position of the twelfth fret coinciding with the point at which the neck crosses the edge of the belly. Plans are available from the suppliers listed at the back of the book.

Cut out a full-sized template for the back of the instrument, and on one half mark in the inner thickness line for the mould and sides. Also, mark in the shape and size of the end blocks, keeping the neck block as the most substantial block of the two. Mark off on some ½ in plywood or block board two identical outlines for the mould, tracing round the inner thickness line of the template. Cut out the moulds. If the work is performed by hand,

rather than by bandsaw, tack both pieces together and square them off with a file or plane.

Cut out the recesses for the blocks. Cut two end blocks and insert them into the recesses, holding them with two glue blocks each.

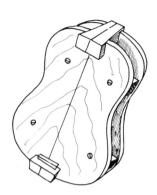

Shape the end blocks as described on page 45 making sure that they adopt the curve of the mould, keeping the line around the side of the mould and blocks sweet and unbroken. Cut the end blocks to length and trim the end grain of the blocks to conform to the swell of the back and the taper of the instrument. Mark and cut the dovetail slot as described on page 155-7.

Cut out the pieces for the neck and the ribs of the guitar. The heel is made from several pieces stacked and glued together and then re-inforced. The ribs or sides are cut from a single piece of clean-grained hardwood. Use the bending iron to help shape the sides, being very careful not to overheat or distort them. If the bending iron illustrated is used, it is a good idea to solder a length of larger diameter copper tube to the end of the bender to prevent intro-ducing local distortions in the sides, which are particularly difficult to remedy.

Fit the sides to the end blocks, holding them to the mould with the rubber bands and half round battens as illustrated. When the joints at the blocks have dried, place the body of the instrument onto a flat board, and screw some simple cams round the perimeter of the instrument. After removing the bands and wooden battens, twist the cams until they press

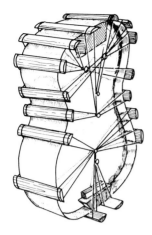

against the sides. Hold them into position until the linings and back are glued in place.

Taper the sides. Fit the linings, leaving them a little proud. Do not alter the linings until the back is shaped. Then the linings can be trimmed down.

The back

Because the back of a classical guitar is rather large and plain, it is common to add some embellishing strips down the centre join. This involves additional and rather tricky work finishing off. If such an inlay is fitted, read ahead to see what is involved before joining the back.

Include the inlay strips at the centre of the back before the back is glued together, so that the inlay is integral with the back board and supported on the inside with a cross-grained reinforcing strip. The banding is made from some straight-grained strips laid on edge between the jointing pieces of the back. Rather than fit a single band down the centre of the back, it is more attractive to make a double strip with a narrow 1/4 in strip of backboard interposed between them. Assemble the back with the battens and wedges in the manner illustrated on page 159, sandwiching the inlay between the larger side boards of the back. Cut a cross-grained reinforcement piece, mark its position on the inside of the back and glue it to cover the area of the joint. When the glue has

dried, chamfer its edges. Rest the sides against the back before cutting the back roughly to size.

Fit the transverse struts as for the mandolin, shaping them where they cross the reinforcement of the back. Fit the back to the sides, trimming the linings and end blocks where necessary, and recessing the ends of the struts into the linings as described on page 163. Glue the back to the sides, holding it down with rubber bands stretched over the back and anchored near the cams holding the sides.

CAM, SCREWED THRO' SPACER TO BASE, AND PRESSED AGAINST SIDE.

181

The belly

Choose close-grained, quarter-sawn softwood
for the belly, and smooth both its inner and
outer face. Plane the surfaces with a shoulder
plane, resting the wood upon some flat,
perfectly clean, ½ in plywood, which will not
distort under the pressure of the tool. Mark the
outline of the belly from the template and check
this against the sides of the instrument before
marking in the centreline and the soundhole.
Inlay the perimeter of the soundhole, either
with an end-grain mosaic or with small pieces
of coloured veneer. Avoid cutting and excavat-
ing the recesses for the inlay too far in advance
of its insertion. By keeping the work in step, the
edges of the recess are less exposed to
accidental damage. Various types of inlay are
available. These can be inserted into the
recesses cut into the perimeter of the soundhole. End-grain inserts give a tighter and neater
finish and show their contrasting colours better
than marquetry.

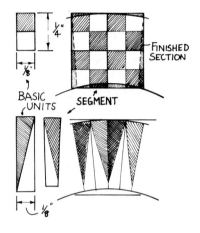

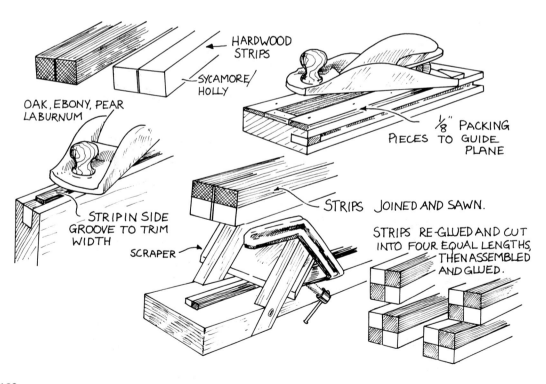

182

You can make simple end-grain patterns fairly easily. Design them to enhance the instrument, not to demonstrate ingenuity and skill. Formulate them in such a way that a single length of stick used twice or four times makes a complete segment of the pattern. It helps to work out the design on graph paper before making the sticks of veneer.

Veneer of differing types and colours is available from the suppliers mentioned at the back of the book. Small quantities of strips made from contrasting woods are easily made and can be levelled to the same thickness using the simple jigs illustrated below.

When assembling these patterns use plenty of glue (carpenters' white PVA glue is ideal for this purpose) to ensure that each strip is firmly bonded into its correct place in the stick. Trim the stick to conform to a segment of the circle into which it is to be inlaid, and support the fragile end-grain while sawing off the inlay

slithers inside a purpose-made saw block. Once the inlay is complete, reinforce the back of the soundhole as described for the mandolin and cut out the circular soundhole using the cutters described on page 161. Round the edges of the soundhole as shown, leaving untouched the area to be covered by the fingerboard.

Fitting the struts

The struts are fitted in the same way as the struts on the mandolin. The additional stiffness they impart helps enhance the tone and responsiveness of the instrument. The upper strut situated beneath the fingerboard ties and strengthens the vulnerably thin belly at the stress point where the belly and the fingerboard meet. Other struts improve the tone of the instrument. Their thickness is judged according to the thickness and resilience of the belly, the lighter sectioned struts being on the bass

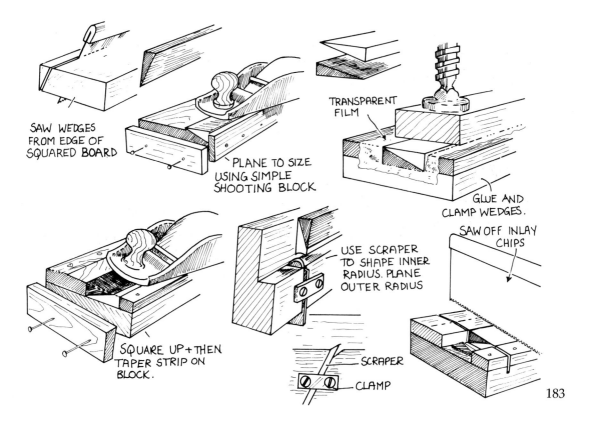

SAW WEDGES FROM EDGE OF SQUARED BOARD

PLANE TO SIZE USING SIMPLE SHOOTING BLOCK

TRANSPARENT FILM

GLUE AND CLAMP WEDGES.

SAW OFF INLAY CHIPS

SQUARE UP + THEN TAPER STRIP ON BLOCK.

USE SCRAPER TO SHAPE INNER RADIUS. PLANE OUTER RADIUS

SCRAPER

CLAMP

183

side of the instrument. Fit the transverse struts first. Clamp them as described on page 163.

The bindings

The bindings are fitted in the same way as described for the mandolin. However, if a decorative double strip has been fitted down the centre of the back, unite the bindings with an inlay strip to achieve a satisfactory decorative effect.

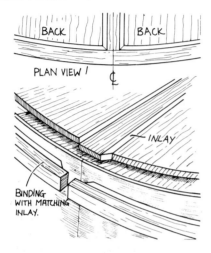

In the same way as the binding rebate was cut in the mandolin, cut around the edges of the guitar. Cut this carefully, stopping the cuts so that the inlay strips down the back of the instrument form neat mitres with the inlay inserted with the binding. Insert the binding

with the inlay immediately, using plenty of glue to ensure that the joints between the sides and the front and the back are not weakened. Hold the bindings with sticky tape. When the glue holding the bindings is dry, remove the tape, carefully peeling it back on itself to prevent lifting the grain, and trim the bindings flush with the sides, back and belly of the guitar.

A second inlay strip can be inserted beneath the bindings on the sides of the guitar at the same time as the bindings are inserted. Terminate these at the bottom of the guitar with neat mitres, joining them to a pair of returns inlaid beside a cross-grained insert down the centre. At the neck, a strip matching the inlay is inserted over the heel and then covered with a capping piece which matches the back as illustrated.

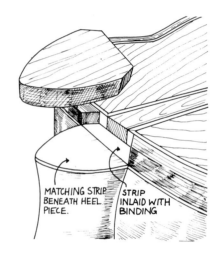

The neck

Use a coping saw and chisel or scalpel to cut away the portion of the belly covering the neck join. Finish shaping with a file. Mark and cut in the angle for the dovetail on the heel. Mark the dovetail and also its shoulders, once the joint face has been established as described for the mandolin on page 154. Approximate the degree to which the shoulders have to be undercut in order to fit tight against the curve of the sides. Incise a shoulder line, relieve it with a chisel and then cut it with the saw.

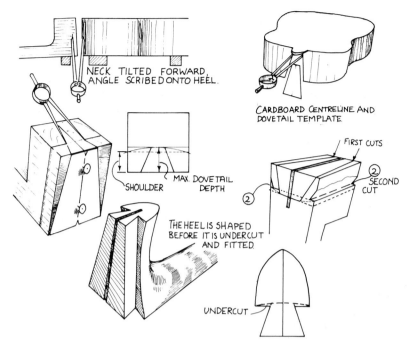

NECK TILTED FORWARD, ANGLE SCRIBED ONTO HEEL.

CARDBOARD CENTRELINE AND DOVETAIL TEMPLATE.

SHOULDER

MAX. DOVETAIL DEPTH

THE HEEL IS SHAPED BEFORE IT IS UNDERCUT AND FITTED.

FIRST CUTS

2 SECOND CUT

2

UNDERCUT

Before undercutting, however, ensure that the heel shaping is virtually complete, otherwise the undercutting may reveal holes when the heel is finished. Whilst fitting the neck, check the centrelines of the guitar to ensure that it remains true. Fit the fingerboard and frets as described for the mandolin and mandola on pages 169-71.

The bridge

Fit the bridge after the nut has been fitted. The bridge should be made from rosewood or ebony. Work the grooves with a plough plane or a simple scratch stock (see below left). Ensure that there is adequate break to the strings. The illustrations show the detail and dimensions of the bridge. The top and edges of the string block can be decorated with bone, ebony or some other combinations of hard materials. Deepen the groove behind the saddle before drilling $1/16$ in string holes. Once the upper work of the bridge is made, trim the

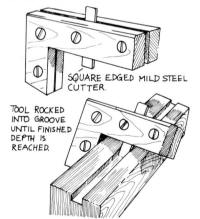

SQUARE EDGED MILD STEEL CUTTER.

TOOL ROCKED INTO GROOVE UNTIL FINISHED DEPTH IS REACHED.

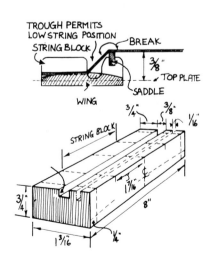

TROUGH PERMITS LOW STRING POSITION

STRING BLOCK

BREAK

$3/8$"

TOP PLATE

SADDLE

WING

STRING BLOCK

$3/4$"

$3/8$"

$1/16$

$7/16$"

8"

$3/4$"

$1\ 3/16$"

$1/4$"

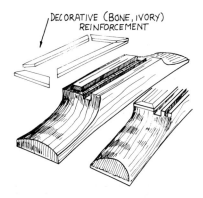

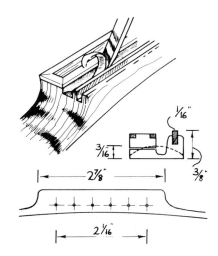

underside of the bridge to fit onto the belly. This will have to be rough shaped, chalked down and glued.

Trim the bridge saddle and the top nut once the instrument is strung up, reducing the string-fret clearance to the minimum possible, but avoiding the rattle that occurs when a depressed string trembles against the adjacent fret. Fasten the strings as illustrated.

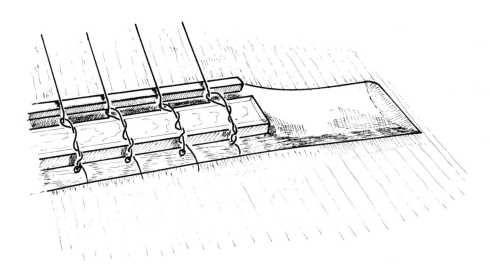

Part VI:

The Jazz Guitar

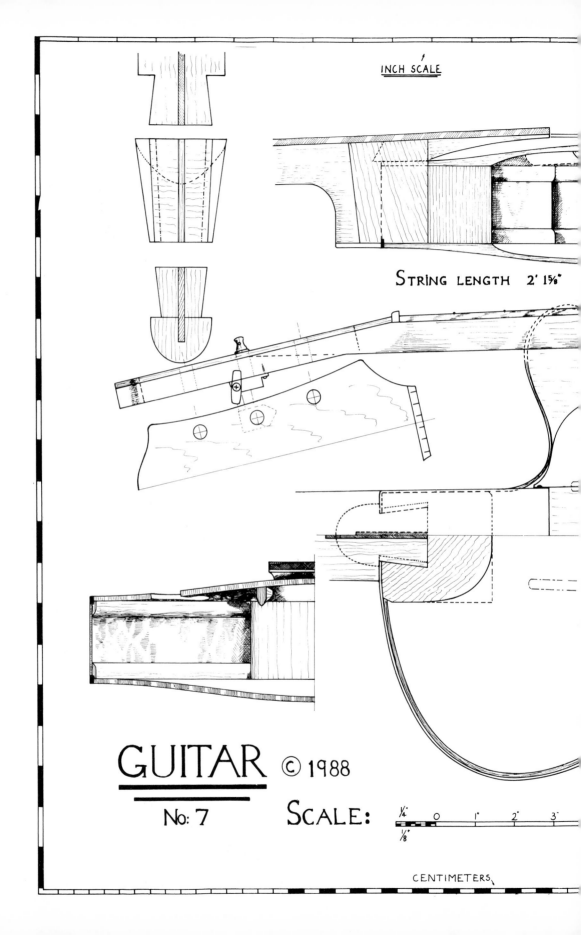

INCH SCALE

STRING LENGTH 2' 1⅝"

GUITAR © 1988

No: 7

SCALE:

¼"

⅛"

0   1"   2"   3"

CENTIMETERS

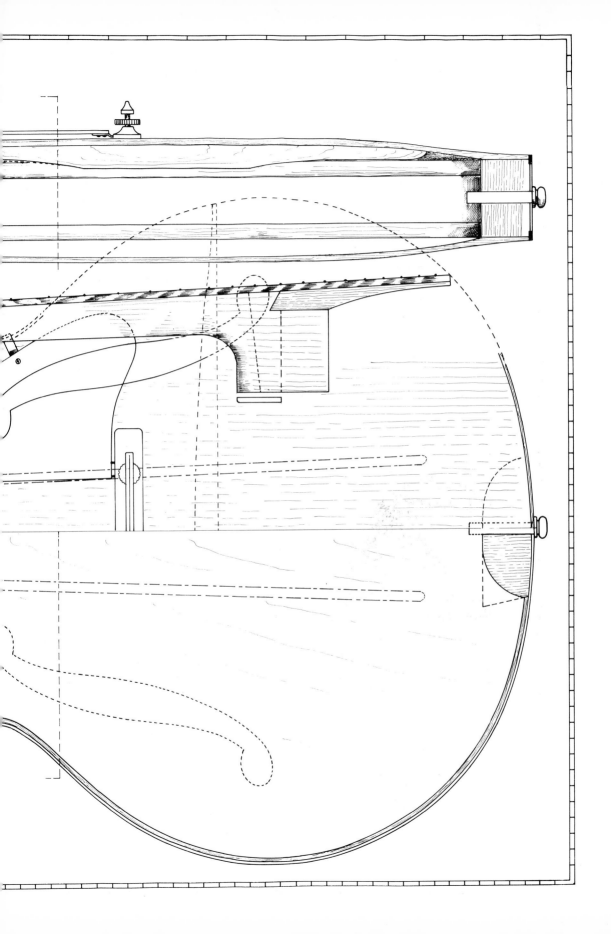

Jazz guitar.

Guitar NO.7 – Construction Sequence

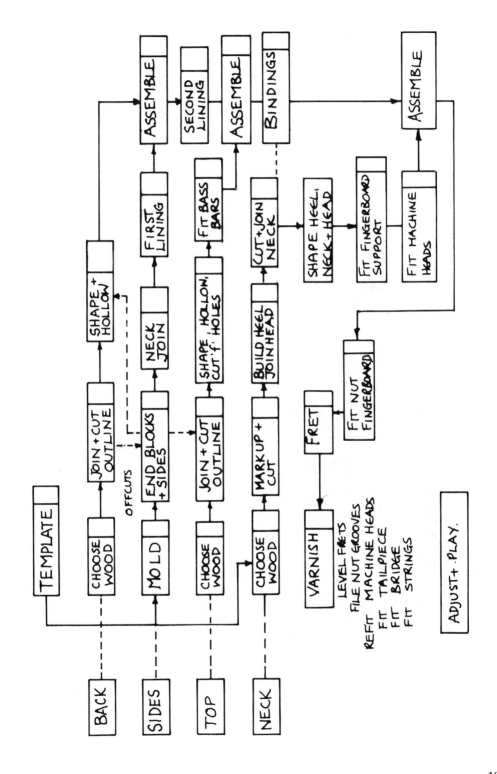

The Jazz Guitar

Jazz guitars are found in a great variety of shapes. This brief section gives instructions for making a slim-bodied semi-acoustic guitar of the style of the late 1950s, with an arched belly and back, an adjustable bridge and a metal tail-piece.

Most of the skills required to make this guitar have already been described in the preceding chapters. Reference will be made to them where the instructions are relevant.

Many of these guitars have moulded ply-wood bellies and backs. If you are not contemplating mass production, it is easier to cut the back and belly from a piece of solid wood and carve it to shape than to set up jigs and moulds for laminating plywood.

Wood

Any of the woods described for any of the instruments will be suitable. Apart from the finish on the fingerboard and belly, these guitars often have opaque or semi-opaque finishes, which enables the maker to use any clean, dry and resonant wood.

The sides

Making the mould

Make a cardboard template of the guitar. At the edge, draw the thickness line for the sides. Mark in the blocks. Because of the narrow sides, the neck block has to be extra strong. Because

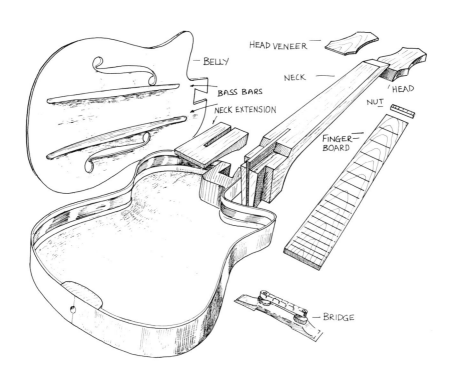

this example illustrated in the plans is asymmetrical, it is impossible to cut one side of the template for the mould and keep the other for the shape of the back and belly. Instead, mark on their respective boards the outlines for the back and belly, then cut the template to make the mould outline.

Screw two pieces of ½ in plywood together and mark on the mouldline, pricking in the sections of the end blocks. Cut out and trim the mould, leaving room for the linings in each side.

Insert the end blocks, hold them with glue blocks and then shape them to the profile of the mould.

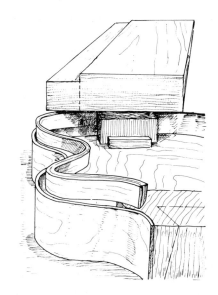

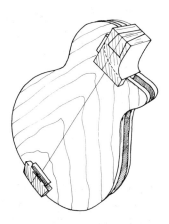

Draw in and cut out a dovetail longer and slightly narrower than that needed for the classical guitar. The instructions for cutting the dovetail are included on page 155.

The sides of the guitar will either be made from a single strip or made from two pieces joined at the end block. Choose straight-grained hardwood, cut on the slab. Cut and plane it to an even thickness as described on page 48 and bend it over the bending iron to fit the mould. Glue and hold the sides in place with elastic bands and wooden strips as before. When the sides are glued into place, fit the first set of linings. The sides do not taper, so once they are in place the linings can be inserted immediately.

Because of the fairly tight curvature, easily

bent ash linings are fitted. These will be best if they are cut on the slab, and bent on the quarter, as illustrated above. There are no transverse struts fitted to the back or belly. The linings in this guitar serve to strengthen the joints at the sides. To help bend the linings, dip them into a bowl of near-boiling water. Dry them with a rag and hold them to the sides with clothespegs. Glue them into place once they are dry and remove their rough edges once the glue has set.

The back

Take the mould and sides, place them over the backboard and check to see whether the outline drawn from the template needs adjustment. Cut out the back and then carve its outer surface in exactly the same way as a violin or cello back is carved, first scribing round the edge of the back and then working towards the area of highest arching. Apart from the curve at the edge of the instrument, try to make all of the shapes convex. See the sections through the back shown in the plans.

Finish the shaping on the outside with the saw rasp, then use scrapers and sandpaper before fitting the back into the shaping box, illustrated and described on page 26. Mark in the position of the linings and the end blocks from the template, and carve out the inside. Do not make the back too thin. An even thickness of 3/16 in is quite satisfactory, although a slight tapering to the sides will enhance its resonance and responsiveness. Finish with the saw rasp, scrapers and sandpaper and fit the back.

The belly

The belly is cut and shaped in the same way. Again a thickness of about 3/16 in is satisfactory. Bore the holes for the f holes before hollowing the instrument. Then cut out the f holes with a knife.

Fitting the sound bars
The sound bars are glued beneath the belly, the one on the treble side being the shorter of the two. Make the bars from quarter-sawn stiff pine, and mark them in and chalk them down as described for the violin. Once they are glued in place, remove the mould and glue the linings and the belly. Fit the bindings and glue them in place as described. These are thinner than those fitted to a classical guitar, because the corners on this guitar are sharper. Bend them against the sides of the belly and back, glue and hold them with clear self-adhesive tape.

The neck

The neck is constructed as illustrated, with additional blocks at the heel to make up the depth, and an extension fitted to the neck, which hangs over the belly. Line up and fit the neck into the dovetail in the neck block. The neck tilts back slightly and this angle is first cut on the heel before the dovetail is cut. Once the neck is fitted, cut back the face of the neck, reinforce it and then insert the fingerboard support which extends over the belly. Fit the head, shave down the face of the neck and veneer the head. Then, with the neck supported on a block, shape the head, neck and heel.

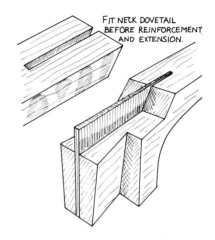

After finishing, fit the neck, machine screws, fingerboard, frets and other fittings. Place the adjustable bridge over the belly, setting each foot over a small spot of Plasticine (modelling clay) and string up the instrument.

Part VII:

Finishing

Finishing

Preparation

Filling dents and bruises

Even the best craftsman will occasionally have to remedy faults and level dents with a filler. For instrument makers the best filler to use is hard wax stopping, obtainable in various colours from the cabinet makers' suppliers listed in the back of this book. Filling with wax stopping is best done when all the colouring is virtually complete. The illustration shows the equipment needed for applying the stopping.

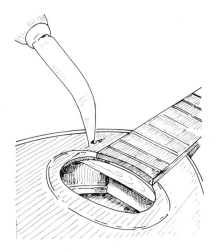

The wax sticks are brittle, and the stopping is applied with a hot knife. Colours are mixed and matched on the point of the knife.

Place the instrument on a soft cloth on the workbench, close to a spirit lamp. Hold the point of the knife in the flame, occasionally testing it for temperature by resting the tip against the side of the stick. When the knife is hot enough, it will melt the wax. Reheat the knife, wipe it clean with fine steel wool and then gently press the point into other sticks to achieve the correct colour mix. Warm the knife and when the wax bubbles, carefully press the

knife into the crevice. If the knife is sufficiently hot, the wax should run easily. Add more until the wax is a little proud of the surface. Clean the knife, warm it and press it against the wax to force it into the wood. Clean off with a chisel when the wax has chilled, finishing with a razor and sandpaper.

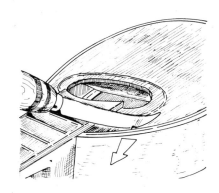

Sanding

Sand the entire instrument before finishing to bring it to a uniform silk-like finish.

Start with 220 grit paper and rest it against a leather strip which has a groove cut in it to bear around the edges of the instrument. Work around the edges, smoothing and rounding the corners and edges. With a new pad, sand the ribs, the belly and the back. On the softwood belly sand slightly across the grain of the board to prevent the sandpaper scouring the softer early wood, leaving the harder late growth high and ribbed.

Follow with 400 grit paper, rubbing over the instrument, taking care to avoid rounding the sharp edges of the scroll and pegbox. Where an instrument incorporates harder woods, use a separate sheet of sandpaper for each wood. Sand the dark woods first, clean off the instrument and then sand the lighter woods using new paper.

Staining

Avoid staining unless the instrument is heavily coloured or ebonized. This is because stains are hard to handle, particularly where there is exposed end grain. The violin, with its arched belly and back and prominent sides, has a lot of end grain which will absorb stain unevenly, leaving the instrument blotchy and ugly. However, it is quite possible to apply a faint base stain to the instrument. This can impart a warm glow beneath the varnish, which is very attractive.

The most commonly used colours are red and yellow. Although commercial woodstains are available, these may be too harsh for the instrument and may include secondary colours which will darken the wood unnecessarily. For the purposes of the instrument maker, home-made stains are recommended. Take some representative wood samples and smooth them to the same finish as the instrument. Select some artists' watercolour paints of the appropriate colour. Check that the colours are permanent and will not fade in strong daylight. Choose transparent colours. Although all good watercolour paints are fairly transparent, some are more translucent than others. For a rich red, Alizaren Crimson is both permanent and clear, and for a yellow either Aurora or Lemon Chrome yellow will do.

Mix up a small quantity of the paint in some warm water, and experiment with the stain on the test pieces, applying it with a flat brush and removing the surplus with a soft rag, wiping it clean in the direction of the grain. When a satisfactory colour has been obtained, giving a clean and faint tint to the samples, mix up a sufficient quantity to colour the instrument.

To hold a violin, push the handle of an oil painting brush or a tapered dowel into the tail pin hole, and hold it by the neck and dowel. Hold other instruments by the neck, and apply the stain evenly onto the belly, sides and back with a soft sponge or brush, wiping away the excess with a cloth. Do not build up too much colour. Leave the violin to dry and then lightly rub the surface with very fine 400 grit paper, and dust it clean.

Violins, violas and cellos

The purpose of the instrument maker is to produce an instrument that both sounds and looks beautiful. It is possible with the aid of modern lacquers and mechanical spray-guns to achieve a perfect finish – one that shines evenly and is smooth and bright, like the finish on a new car. For these instruments, the finish should be a subtle lustre rather than a high polish, with perhaps slight variations of colour and tone over the body and neck.

To help gain experience in the beauties of the different types of finish, visit music shops which sell new, factory-made, instruments, and inspect their finish. Then, for a contrast, look at some older instruments, perhaps in private ownership or in exhibition. In this context, a visit to the Hill's Instrument Collection in the Ashmolean Museum, Oxford to see the Amati and Stradivarius violins and other masterpieces there, is well worthwhile.

The finishing schedule described here is a slow and gradual process, and one which is always open to alteration and adaption. Like an oil painting, it can be worked up or taken back, until the desired effect is achieved.

Violin varnishes are based on a combination of resins and linseed oil and are slow-drying.

Heat and ventilation help to accelerate drying, sunlight or strong ultra-violet light dramatically speed drying. Because of this, it is necessary to find a fairly dust-free area, where the instrument can hang in the sunlight, or at least in clear daylight, and where it can remain fairly cool so that the instrument is not warped by heat accumulated during a prolonged exposure to the sun.

I have made a simple cubicle in the cellar and equipped it with an ultra-violet lamp, so that even in the winter I am able to dry violin and cello varnish. For the spring, summer and autumn, a well-ventilated greenhouse or conservatory is ideal, where the instruments can dangle on strings and rotate slowly in a slight draught. The air flow and the slight movement prevent distortions owing to localized overheating.

Establish the colour of the instrument first and add tonal variations in later coats.

Choose a fairly dark varnish, which, when the bottle is held to the light, promises to give the desired colour. Decant a small quantity and thin it slightly with turpentine. Then, hold the instrument by the neck, and with the bottom supported on the dowel stuck into the tail pin hole, work the varnish into the back, the sides and the belly with a stiff, clean oil colour brush. Leave the instrument to dry and then scrape the varnish right back to the wood with a sharp razor, working with a very short scraping action, taking great care not to scratch the instrument. Apply an unthinned second coat and clean it off when the varnish has dried. Continue to apply and scrape off the varnish with a razor for several coats. Each time a very thin layer of varnish is left and the colour of the instrument slowly darkens.

Once the grain has been filled and the surface sealed, the shading and, if necessary, the ageing can be applied. To reach this stage, at least three coats of varnish will have been applied and cleaned back. Inspect the surface of the instrument. If it is sealed, it will shine with a slight lustre.

Shading

Shading and antique marks can be applied at this stage by mixing a very small quantity of artists' oil colour with the varnish and painting in the tonal variations and the age marks. It is very important that a transparent paint should be used. Burnt sienna, for instance, is a much cleaner and more translucent colour than burnt umber, although, as colours, both might be suitable. Choose colours which are clear and, if possible, identical to the colour of the instrument.

Squirt small quantities of artists' oil colours at the perimeter of a clean plate, and make a small pool of unthinned varnish in the middle. With a stiff oil painting brush, mix the varnish with the pigments and brush the colour straight onto the violin. At no point should the shading be opaque. Vary the proportions of oil paint to varnish at various points of the instrument. Colour and tonal variations must be subtle. Shade the areas between the f holes and the inner bouts, the areas beneath the fingerboard and the tailpiece, and also at the corners and round the sides. Wipe and dab with small pads made from offcuts of chamois leather to help fade and tone in the shading.

Leave the violin to dry and then smooth the surface with a razor. Continue with additional coats of varnish, adding tone and colour from the palette where necessary, and cleaning back between coats with the razor. Continue with more coats of varnish, where necessary, adding tone and colour with each coat. With this system there is always an opportunity for the maker to alter and improve his work. As the coats build up and the desired effects are achieved, use the razor more and more lightly. On the last coats, when the finish is smooth and regular, use the razor to remove remaining bumps and undulations.

Follow with fine 400 grit paper, lubricated with a drop of olive oil and then wipe clean; leave the instrument for a day or two to dry. Rub over the surface with fine steel wool (0000) to even the finish. Dust it.

Take a white cotton handkerchief, and apply the smallest quantity of olive oil to one corner and a small spot of methylated spirits to the opposite corner. Rub the corners together and bundle them into a small pad. Vigorously rub the back, belly and the sides. This burnishes and pulls the varnish over. Wipe the surface dry after an hour. Leave the violin for two or three days, then take a bottle of benzoin resin which has been dissolved in spirits, and tip a very small quantity onto one corner of the handkerchief and olive oil on the other. Lightly, but with increasing pressure, rub the back, sides and belly to give a bright finish coat of benzoin resin, which shines and imparts a beautiful smell to the instrument.

An alternative method of finishing off the varnishing is to apply a last coat of varnish, and then when it is thoroughly dry, rub it down with 400 grit paper. Then grind the surfaces with a leather pad dipped in a pan of pumice powder and water. Leave the instrument for a couple of days and then follow with a new pad, dipped in rottenstone powder and water. Clean off, then follow with an abrasive car polish, applied with a soft rag.

Problems

Nearly all of the problems that occur using the above methods are caused by the varnish not being dry enough. The varnish must dry before new coats are applied, otherwise it will be impossible to work the surface to a smooth and even finish. Do not try to rush the finishing process.

This varnish must be thin enough for the ultra-violet light rays to penetrate before drying really begins. With pigment added to an already dark varnish, the thicker the varnish is, the more efficiently it will filter out the U.V. rays and delay drying.

Burning the surface when rubbing down
If there is too much alcohol applied with the cloth, the varnish will be torn by the action of the solvent. Use only the very smallest quantity of the methylated spirits and dilute it with olive oil. Also, even though the methylated spirits will evaporate quickly, the benzoin resin will still be soft, and must be left for a day before final polishing.

The neck
A harder, quicker drying shellac or varnish should be used for the neck and scroll. The techniques for applying it are the same as those described above. Shellac varnish is coloured using spirit-soluble stains, which come in the form of a fine, concentrated powder. Dissolve the powder in methylated or finishing spirit until the correct colour is achieved, then strain the liquid before pouring into the shellac, stir, and leave the shellac to thicken by evaporation before applying it.

Because the neck and the scroll constitute a small proportion of the instrument, avoid adding too much shading to this part, otherwise it will seem darker than the rest of the instrument when the fingerboard and the pegs are fitted.

Mandolins and guitars

The finishing schedule described in the previous section is recommended for these instruments too. However, if you want a harder and brighter finish on your instruments, the following finishing system will be useful.

Sand and stain the instrument as described, lightly rubbing down between applications of stain, and stopping the staining before the different take-up of the wood is revealed in a patchiness in the finish – stop when you have a uniform tone over the whole body, taking care not to apply too much tone to the end grain.

Apply a shellac-based sanding sealer. This is a quick-drying sealer. Shake it before use, then apply it by brush in quick strokes, following the grain of the wood. Leave the shellac to dry, and then rub down the surface again and clear away the dust with a soft brush.

Add more stain and colour if necessary. Then apply a second sealing coat and rub down as before.

Use a catalyst lacquer for the finish coats. This should be mixed and applied according to the makers' instructions and applied in a warm and dust-free room.

Apply the first coat with a mop or soft brush, and leave it for a day to dry. Level the surfaces with fine paper, backed against a slightly flexible leather pad. Wipe clean. Build up a finish, cutting back between coats, until there is a sufficient thickness of lacquer to risk cutting back to a smooth and level polish. Bringing a bright glitter to a finish is mainly accomplished by sanding and grinding away all surface irregularities; if the major bumps are eliminated early in the finishing process there should be only a few small bumps and innumerable tiny ones to remove. Therefore, avoid using a sandpaper at this stage, which will itself scratch the finish deeper than the pimples and spots you are trying to remove.

After four or five coats of lacquer, there should be enough finish to work back a polish. Leave the instrument for a week or so until the finish is fully cured, then work back the surfaces, using first 400 grit paper or a very fine wet and dry paper. Follow with pumice and then a burnishing cream, applied with a leather pad. Take care when rubbing back, because although there may be plenty of finish on the level surfaces, the corners may be less well covered. They certainly receive far more pressure from the rubbing pad, and the finish there will be cut back very quickly. So concentrate on the large flat surfaces, only venturing to the edge when the others are smooth and bright.

Clean the instrument with a soft rag, and if the finish ever needs reviving, burnish it with a soft cloth or polish it with a car wax polish.

Index